THE SLOWCOOKER LIBRARY

Real Meals from your Slow Cooker

Annette Yates and Wendy Hobson

foulsham

LONDON • NEW YORK • TORONTO • SYDNEY

foulsham

The Oriel, Thames Valley Court, 183–187 Bath Road, Slough, Berkshire SL1 4AA, England

Foulsham books can be found in all good bookshops and direct from www.foulsham.com

ISBN: 978-0-572-03540-2

Copyright © 2010 W. Foulsham & Co. Ltd

Cover photograph © Food Features

A CIP record for this book is available from the British Library

Printed in Dubai

contents

introduction

For those of us with no time to spend cooking when we get home from work, slow cookers fit perfectly into our busy lifestyles. Just prepare the ingredients and place them in your slow cooker before leaving home and return to a delicious hot meal. Plus the meals are ready when you are; because of the time range, there is little chance of them spoiling even if you are an hour or two late.

A slow cooker can be used day or night; cook tomorrow's lunch or breakfast overnight, for example. Use the slow cooker while you are out, or while you are at home, and appreciate both the freedom of knowing that a delicious and nutritious meal is cooking itself and the satisfaction of economising on fuel. Some of the recipes have all-day cooking times, but others have shorter cooking times for a mid-day meal or when you simply want to get on with something else while your dinner cooks itself!

Your slow cooker also makes an ideal companion to your freezer as it is simple to use it for larger quantities than usual, then freeze some to use at a later date.

The following recipes provide a selection of interesting and tasty ideas for your slow cooker. But don't stop there: use the recipes as a basis to experiment and develop your own favourite ideas so that your range of delicious meals never stops expanding.

choosing a slow cooker

Always choose a cooker that bears the BEAB safety symbol, which will have a removable pot for ease of use (some older slow cookers had a fixed pot). All slow cookers should have a well-fitting lid, which will be either heat-resistant glass or stoneware. It is not necessarily an advantage to have a glass lid as the condensation will block your view of the cooking food anyway. The main heat settings available are High and Low, which are what you need for the recipes in this book, but many models also now have Medium, and some also have an automatic function and an auto shut-off.

Choose a slow cooker with sufficient capacity for your specific needs and consider whether you will use it for entertaining or for making extra quantities for the freezer. If you regularly cook for one, then a smaller capacity will be fine, but if you cook for four or more, own a freezer or entertain on a regular basis, look for a 3 litre/5¼ pt capacity. A cooker with a wide bowl will be easier to use for ingredients such as (bell) peppers, fish or whole fruit.

advantages of slow cooking

There are many advantages to slow cooking, especially for those who have better things to do than slave over a hot stove! Saving time may be top of your list of advantages, or perhaps the flexibility to cook when you want to and have a hot meal ready whenever you want to eat, but there are plenty of other positive features of slow cooking.

Slow cookers are superb for preparing soups, stocks, casseroles and stews. Flavours blend and develop to produce concentrated, rich and tasty results as all the flavours are sealed in the pot. The slow cooking method tenderises even the toughest cuts of meat and prevents shrinkage of joints.

You are not only saving time and effort but there are also considerable fuel economies with this cooking method. Fuel savings alone can be as much as 80 per cent on normal cooking times. The efficient built-in insulation means only the food inside the slow cooker heats up, not the whole kitchen.

The gentle heat results in less evaporation of liquids so there is little chance of food drying out. The steam condenses on the lid and returns to the pot. In doing so it forms a seal that retains heat and flavour, which avoids steaming up the kitchen and filling it with cooking smells, losing valuable nutrients, and having to top up the steaming water for puddings! This makes the slow cooker ideal for cooking light sponges and steaming smooth pâtés.

Foods cooked in the slow cooker remain attractively whole – a distinct advantage when cooking fruit, fish and other ingredients. There is no need to turn or stir the food as it is not likely to overcook, boil over or stick and there are no hot spots to cause burning.

Once cooking is complete, food can safely be kept on the low setting for several hours without spoiling – making it perfect for families who do not all want to eat their meal at the same time.

advantages of slow cooking

preparation & cooking

Always follow the manufacturer's instructions carefully when connecting the slow cooker to the power supply. The appliance must be earthed. As different models will vary slightly, always check your instruction booklet for the usage instructions of your particular cooker. These basic rules are appropriate to all types.

Preparing food

- Always ensure that frozen ingredients are properly thawed at room temperature before cooking.

- Vegetables take longer to cook than meat as they normally cook at higher temperatures. They should therefore be thinly sliced or diced into 5 mm/¼ in pieces and placed near the bottom of the slow cooker (the hottest point), covered in the cooking liquid. If you are browning the meat for a recipe, sauté the vegetables for a few minutes at the same time. Completely thaw frozen vegetables, then add them during the final hour of cooking.

- Use quick-cooking varieties of pasta or rice and add to the dish for the last 30 minutes of cooking. Soften macaroni and lasagne in boiling water for a few minutes before cooking and make sure they are immersed in liquid. Extra liquid is needed when using raw rice: use 150 ml/¼ pt/⅔ cup for 100 g/4 oz/½ cup of rice. No additional liquid is required when slow cooking cooked rice.

- If using dried beans, soak them overnight in cold water, then bring to the boil in fresh water and boil rapidly for 15 minutes before draining and using in the recipe. This will destroy any natural toxins found in the beans.

- Use seasoning and flavouring ingredients sparingly as most of their flavour is retained during cooking. If in doubt, season lightly, then adjust the seasoning of the finished dish.

using your slow cooker

1 Preheat the slow cooker if necessary, with the lid on. You can assemble, prepare and brown the ingredients while the slow cooker is heating.

2 Browning ingredients before placing them in the slow cooker can improve the appearance of the finished dish. Fry prepared meat in a little oil in a frying pan until browned, then add the prepared vegetables and fry until softened and starting to brown.

3 If you are using thickening agents, such as flour or cornflour (cornstarch), toss the pieces of meat in the flour before adding them to the frying pan, or stir them into the browning ingredients and stir until browned. If you have not added a thickening agent at the start of cooking, mix the flour or cornflour with a little cold water and stir it into the ingredients for the final 1–1½ hours of cooking.

4 Transfer the ingredients to the slow cooker using a slotted spoon so that they come to within 1–2 cm/½–¾ in of the top of the earthenware pot. Stir in any seasonings.

5 Never leave uncooked food in the slow cooker to be switched on later or store a removable slow cooker pot in the fridge. If necessary, store prepared ingredients in a separate container in the fridge.

6 Always mix ingredients together well to prevent foods from sticking together.

7   Replace the lid and select the recommended heat setting. Where recipes recommend cooking on High for 20–30 minutes before turning to Low, you can use the Auto setting instead, if available.

8   Leave the slow cooker undisturbed during the cooking period and keep the lid on, otherwise the water seal around the rim will be broken and it will take a considerable time to regain the lost heat.

9   Stir soups and casseroles well before serving.

10 Once cooking is completed and the servings for that occasion have been used, transfer any remaining food from the slow cooker, cool quickly, then chill or freeze.

One-step slow cooking

In the one-step method, the cold ingredients are placed directly into the slow cooker. You can use this method if you prefer not to brown food or if you are short of preparation time.

1   Always preheat the slow cooker.

2   Make sure that fresh vegetables are diced finely and place them in the slow cooker before adding the meat or poultry and seasoning ingredients, then pour over enough boiling water to cover all the ingredients.

3   Mix the thickening agent with a little cold water to form a paste and stir in with the ingredients. Alternatively, coat the meat with flour before adding it to the slow cooker. When the thickening agent is tomato purée (paste) or condensed soup, ensure these are mixed well with the other ingredients.

4   Add at least 3 hours on Low to recipe times if you are cooking by the one-step method.

hints & tips

- Heat settings can often be adjusted to suit your lifestyle. Generally, the cooking time on High is just over half that on Low.
- Steamed dishes, recipes that include a raising agent and recipes with large pieces of meat should always be cooked on High.
- If steaming a pudding in a bowl or basin, fold a strip of foil and place it underneath the basin, then fold the strip over the top. When the pudding is finished, you will more easily be able to lift out the basin using the strip of foil.
- Avoid direct draughts and low room temperatures while cooking as these will affect the slow cooker. Allow slightly longer cooking times if the room is likely to be cold, especially when cooking on Low.
- Recipe cooking times can be affected by variations in electricity supply. If the recipe is not ready at the end of the cooking time, replace the lid and cook for at least another hour on High.
- Cooked food should not be reheated in the slow cooker.
- Add milk and cream to savoury dishes during the final 30 minutes since long cooking could cause them to separate.
- If your slow cooker has a removable pot, cooked dishes can be browned under the grill (broiler) or covered with a topping and crisped in a preheated oven.
- Add dumplings to soups or stews for the final 30 minutes and switch to the High setting.
- Dry cooking is not recommended since it could cause damage to your slow cooker.

- If portions are to be eaten by latecomers, leave them in the slow cooker on Low.

- Remember that the temperature of a slow cooker on High does not compare with even the lowest setting in a conventional oven, so be careful when adapting conventional recipes. When adapting recipes for slow cooking, use about half the normal quantity of liquid since there is less evaporation.

- Food that is not to be eaten straight away should always be cooled quickly before chilling or freezing. The slow cooker will retain heat for some time, so do not leave food in the slow cooker.

notes on the recipes

- The recipes in this book have been tested in a range of slow cookers. However, models do vary, so you may find it helpful to compare the cooking time of a recipe with a similar one in your own manufacturer's instruction book.
- Do not mix metric, imperial and American measures. Follow one set only.
- American terms are given in brackets.
- All spoon measurements are level: 1 tsp = 5 ml; 1 tbsp = 15 ml.
- Eggs are medium unless otherwise stated. If you use a different size, adjust the amount of liquid added to obtain the right consistency.
- Always wash, peel, core and seed, if necessary, fresh fruit and vegetables before use.
- Seasoning and the use of strongly flavoured ingredients, such as onions and garlic, is very much a matter of personal taste. Slow cooked recipes tend to need less seasoning as the flavour is concentrated during the long cooking time, so taste the food and adjust the seasoning as necessary.
- Always use fresh herbs unless dried are specifically called for. If you wish, you can substitute dried for fresh, using only half the quantity or less as they are very pungent, but chopped frozen varieties are much better than dried. There is no substitute for fresh parsley and coriander (cilantro).
- Use any good-quality oil, like sunflower, corn or groundnut (peanut), unless olive oil is called for.

- A fresh bouquet garni is traditionally made up of sprigs of thyme, parsley and a bay leaf tied together with string or wrapped in muslin (cheesecloth) and is used in slow-cooked dishes. Sachets of dried bouquet garni are readily available in supermarkets.
- Use butter or a margarine of your choice in the recipes. Since some margarines or spreads are best for particular uses, check the packet before using for the first time.
- Use your own discretion in substituting ingredients and personalising the recipes. Make notes of particular successes as you go along.
- Use whichever kitchen gadgets you like to speed up preparation and cooking times: mixers for whisking, food processors for grating, slicing, mixing or kneading, blenders for liquidising.
- Cooking times are approximate. If you alter the quantities of the recipe, the cooking times will vary only slightly because of the nature of the cooking method.
- Follow the preheating instructions for your own model of slow cooker. Preheat your slow cooker while you are assembling and preparing the ingredients.
- Serving suggestions are ideas only – use your own imagination!
- The icons on the recipes indicate:

SERVING

PREPARATION TIME

COOKING TIME

SERVE WITH

soups

Ideal for the slow cooker, there's no worries about leaving your home-made soups for a few hours longer than the recommended cooking time. The results will still be delicious, perfectly cooked and tasty, the flavours from each ingredient having developed and intermingled gently for hours. The soups included in this section can be served as substantial starters, or accompanied by some crusty bread to make a meal in themselves.

If you can, use your leftover vegetables and bones to make stock in your slow cooker, as it will be concentrated and full of flavour and will make the perfect base for soups, stews and casseroles.

Soup tips

- Remember that vegetables take longer to cook than meat so should be finely diced.

- Browning the ingredients before slow cooking will add extra flavour and colour to the finished soup.

- Season with care, and preferably after cooking, as slow-cooked soups retain more of their own concentrated flavours and therefore require less seasoning.

- If you use flour or cornflour (cornstarch) to thicken soups, add them at the start of the cooking time or for the final $1\frac{1}{2}$ hours (see page 12).

- If you are using cream, milk or egg yolks to thicken a soup, add them for only the last 30 minutes of cooking.

- Use a good-quality chicken or vegetable stock.

- There is very little loss of liquid during cooking, so when adapting your own recipes, halve the amount of liquid added. You can also top up with boiling water once the dish is ready.

- Freeze cold soup in sealed polythene containers. Stock can be frozen in ice-cube bags so you can use it in small quantities when you need it in your cooking.

beef or chicken stock

1.75 litres/ 3 pts/7½ cups   **10 MINS**   **10-16 hrs LOW**

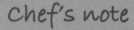

Chef's note

You can buy stock from the chill cabinet, or use stock cubes, but your own home-made stock has to be the best and the slow cooker can't be beaten as a way of making it. Don't worry about quantities – use what vegetables you have – but go easy on any strongly flavoured items. Once made, cool it quickly and refrigerate, or freeze it in small quantities so it is convenient to use.

1.75 kg/4 lb raw or cooked **bones or poultry carcass**

1 **onion**, chopped

1 **carrot**, chopped

1 **celery stick**, chopped

Salt

Whole black peppercorns

1 **bouquet garni** sachet

Boiling water

1   Preheat the slow cooker on High.

2   Break up the bones as small as possible to extract the most flavour. Place all the ingredients in the slow cooker with sufficient boiling water to cover.

3   Cook on Low for 10–16 hours.

4   Discard the bouquet garni. Strain the stock and leave to cool.

5   Skim off any surface fat and chill or freeze.

freezing tip
• Freeze in small quantities ready for use – ice-cube bags are handy.

traditional beef broth

6-8

10
MINS

6-10hrs
LOW

Chef's note

One of the best-ever comfort foods, full of goodness and flavour and guaranteed to warm you through on a winter's day. The pearl barley is a traditional ingredient that thickens and adds texture to make a satisfying, filling broth.

15 ml/1 tbsp **oil**

225 g/8 oz **stewing steak**, finely chopped

2 **onions**, diced

225 g/8 oz **carrots**, diced

225 g/8 oz **potatoes**, diced

1 **leek**, thinly sliced

20 ml/4 tsp **plain (all-purpose) flour**

1.2 litres/2 pts/5 cups **beef stock**

25 g/1 oz **pearl barley**

Salt and freshly ground black pepper

1   Preheat the slow cooker on High.

2   Heat the oil in a frying pan and fry the meat gently until browned on all sides. Transfer to the slow cooker.

3   Add the vegetables to the pan and fry gently for 3–4 minutes.

4   Stir in the flour, then gradually add the stock, stirring well. Add the pearl barley and seasoning. Bring to the boil, then transfer to the slow cooker and stir well.

5   Cook on Low for 6–10 hours.

6   Stir well and adjust the seasoning before serving.

chicken broth

• Prepare as for **beef broth**, but substitute chicken meat and chicken stock for the beef.

split pea and bacon soup

6-8

10 MINS

8-10hrs LOW

Crusty bread

Chef's note

Split peas, like all pulses, are an economical source of protein and are very good for you. A packet will keep for a very long time in your storecupboard – but when you want to use them in a recipe you do have to remember to allow for the essential soaking time.

225 g/8 oz/1⅓ cups **split peas**

5 ml/1 tsp **bicarbonate of soda** (baking soda)

25 g/1 oz/2 tbsp **butter or margarine**

4 **streaky bacon** rashers (slices), rinded and chopped

1 **leek**, chopped

1 **celery** stick, chopped

1 litre/1¾ pts/4¼ cups **chicken stock**

5 ml/1 tsp **dried mixed herbs**

Salt and freshly ground black pepper

1   Soak the split peas in plenty of cold water with the bicarbonate of soda for 5–6 hours or overnight.

2   Preheat the slow cooker on High.

3   Heat the butter or margarine in a frying pan and fry the bacon, leek and celery for 3–4 minutes. Transfer to the slow cooker.

4   Strain the split peas, then stir them into the slow cooker with the stock and herbs. Season with salt and pepper.

5   Cook on Low for 8–10 hours.

6   Purée or mash the soup well, then reheat.

7   Serve with crusty bread.

serving tip
• This soup is also lovely served with dumplings.

french onion soup

Chef's note

A warming soup when you have a glut of onions, or a great starter for a dinner party. The last-minute addition of the cheese on toast adds a traditional touch and is quick and easy.

 **6**

 **10** MINS

 **6-8** hrs LOW

 Crusty bread

40 g/1½ oz/3 tbsp **butter or margarine**

700 g/1½ lb **onions**, thinly sliced

1 litre/1¾ pts/4¼ cups **chicken stock**

1 **bay leaf**

Salt and freshly ground black pepper

½ **baguette**, thickly sliced

225 g/8 oz/2 cups **strong cheese**, grated

1. Preheat the slow cooker on High.

2. Heat the butter or margarine in a frying pan and fry the onions gently until golden brown.

3. Stir in the stock, add the bay leaf and season with salt and pepper. Bring to the boil, then transfer to the slow cooker.

4. Cook on Low for 6–8 hours. Discard the bay leaf.

5. If you want a smooth consistency, purée the soup, then reheat to serve.

6. Sprinkle the baguette slices with the cheese and grill (broil) under a hot grill (broiler) until melted.

7. Serve the soup in warmed bowls and float the bread and cheese slices on top.

cream of onion soup

• Prepare as for **french onion soup**, but after puréeing stir in 150 ml/ ¼ pt/⅔ cup of double (heavy) cream to the puréed mixture and reheat without allowing the soup to boil.

lentil soup
with bacon

6   **10** MINS   **6-8** hrs LOW   Wholemeal bread

25 g/1 oz/2 tbsp **butter or margarine**

4 **bacon rashers** (slices), rinded and chopped

2 **onions**, chopped

2 **carrots**, chopped

2 **celery sticks**, chopped

1.2 litres/2 pts/5 cups **water**

15 ml/1 tbsp **tomato purée** (paste)

1 **bouquet garni** sachet

225 g/8 oz/1⅓ cups **lentils**

1　Preheat the slow cooker on High.

2　Heat the butter or margarine in a frying pan and fry the bacon, onions, carrots and celery gently for 3–4 minutes.

3　Add the remaining ingredients and bring to the boil, then transfer to the slow cooker.

4　Cook on Low for 6–8 hours. Discard the bouquet garni.

5　Purée the soup or rub through a sieve (strainer), then reheat.

6　Serve with wholemeal bread.

cook's tip
• If you rub the soup through a sieve you'll get a smoother texture.

fresh tomato soup

Chef's note

Tomato soup is often served at firework parties – but then it's usually from a can and served in a mug to enjoy around the bonfire. Nothing beats the full flavour of home-made, though, whether you make the clearer, thinner soup or the creamed version.

25 g/1 oz/2 tbsp **butter or margarine**

1 **onion**, finely chopped

1 **carrot**, finely chopped

2 **celery sticks**, finely chopped

4 **streaky bacon** rashers (slices), rinded and chopped

700 g/1½ lb **tomatoes**, skinned

900 ml/1½ pts/3¾ cups **chicken stock**

5 ml/1 tsp **caster (superfine) sugar**

a large pinch of **dried mixed herbs**

Salt and freshly ground black pepper

1   Preheat the slow cooker on High.

2   Heat the butter or margarine in a frying pan and fry the onion, carrot, celery and bacon gently for 3–4 minutes.

3   Stir in the remaining ingredients and bring to the boil, then transfer to the slow cooker.

4   Cook on Low for 8–10 hours.

5   Stir well before serving. Alternatively, purée the soup for a smooth consistency.

6   Serve with crusty rolls.

cream of tomato soup

• Prepare as for **fresh tomato soup**, but after puréeing stir in 150 ml/ ¼ pt/⅔ cup of double (heavy) cream and reheat without allowing the soup to boil.

fresh watercress soup

4-6

10 MINS

6-8 hrs LOW

Tomato ciabatta

Chef's note

This soup has a vibrantly green colour and a smooth, velvety texture. Watercress is a wonderfully healthy ingredient, containing both iron and the vitamin C needed to help your body absorb this essential mineral. Use vegetable stock instead of chicken if you want to make a vegetarian version.

50 g/2 oz/¼ cup **butter or margarine**

1 **onion**, finely chopped

1 **garlic clove**, crushed

2 bunches of **watercress**

600 ml/1 pt/2½ cups **chicken stock**

Salt and freshly ground black pepper

300 ml/½ pt/1¼ cups **milk**

1   Preheat the slow cooker on High.

2   Heat the butter or margarine in a frying pan and fry the onion and garlic until transparent.

3   Reserve a few small watercress sprigs for garnish, then stir in the remainder and cook for a further 2–3 minutes, stirring all the time.

4   Add the stock and seasoning and bring to the boil, then transfer to the slow cooker.

5   Cook on Low for 6–8 hours.

6   Purée the soup, then stir in the milk and reheat.

7   Garnish each bowl with the reserved sprigs of watercress.

8   Serve with tomato ciabatta or your favourite bread.

freezing tip

• Make and purée the soup without adding the milk, then cool and freeze the soup in a rigid container. Stir in the milk when reheating.

spinach & celery soup

6 · **10** MINS · **6-10**hrs LOW · Melba toast

Chef's note

This is a combination you might not have thought of before, but spinach and celery really do work wonderfully together. The swirl of cream is very attractive, but you could grate a little fresh nutmeg over each serving too for decoration and extra flavour, if liked.

---

25 g/1 oz/2 tbsp **butter or margarine**

1 small head of **celery**, chopped

1 **onion**, chopped

450 g/1 lb **spinach**, roughly chopped

900 ml/1½ pts/3¾ cups **water**

Salt and freshly ground black pepper

150 ml/¼ pt/⅔ cup **milk**

90 ml/6 tbsp **double (heavy) cream**

1   Preheat the slow cooker on High.

2   Heat the butter or margarine in a large frying pan and fry the celery and onion gently for a few minutes.

3   Add the spinach, water and salt and pepper and bring to the boil. Boil just until the spinach begins to wilt slightly, then transfer to the slow cooker.

4   Cook on Low for 6–10 hours.

5   Purée the soup, stir in the milk and reheat. Swirl 15 ml/1 tbsp of cream in each bowl and serve.

6   Serve with melba toast.

freezing tip

• Make and purée the soup without adding the milk, then cool and freeze the soup in a rigid container. Stir in the milk when reheating.

winter vegetable soup

6   **15** MINS   **6-10** hrs LOW   **Baked potatoes**

Chef's note

This recipe is proof that you can make wonderfully appetising soup from the most basic of ingredients. We suggest serving it with baked potatoes, but it also goes well with chunks of rustic bread or crusty rolls.

50 g/2 oz/¼ cup **butter or margarine**

2 **onions**, chopped

225 g/8 oz **carrots**, diced

225 g/8 oz **parsnips**, diced

2 **celery sticks**, chopped

225 g/8 oz **tomatoes**, skinned and chopped

30 ml/2 tbsp **plain (all-purpose) flour**

1 litre/1¾ pts **vegetable stock**

1 **bouquet garni** sachet

Salt and freshly ground black pepper

1 Preheat the slow cooker on High.

2 Heat the butter or margarine in a frying pan and fry the onions, carrots, parsnips and celery gently for about 5 minutes.

3 Stir in the tomatoes.

4 Mix the flour with a little cold stock to form a smooth paste, then stir this into the pan with the remaining stock and the bouquet garni and mix well. Season with salt and pepper. Bring to the boil, then transfer to the slow cooker.

5 Cook on Low for 6–10 hours. Discard the bouquet garni.

6 Serve with baked potatoes.

serving tip

• Sprinkle the baked potatoes with grated cheese to make a more filling meal.

creamed seafood soup

4-6

10 MINS

5 hrs
4 HIGH +
1 LOW

Crusty bread

Chef's note

A very special soup that is ideal as a first course when entertaining. The richness and smoothness come from making a purée with the potato and milk.

3 streaky **bacon rashers** (slices), rinded and chopped

1 **onion**, sliced

2 **potatoes**, diced

700 g/1½ lb **cod fillets**, cut into chunks

300 ml/½ pt/1¼ cups **fish stock**

Salt and freshly ground black pepper

150 ml/¼ pt/⅔ cup **milk**

50 g/2 oz **cooked, peeled prawns (shrimp)**

1   Preheat the slow cooker on High.

2   Fry the bacon and onion in a frying pan until soft and transparent.

3   Add the potatoes and fry for a further 5 minutes, then transfer to the slow cooker, add the fish and stock and season with salt and pepper.

4   Cook on High for 3–4 hours.

5   Purée the soup, then stir in the milk and prawns and cook on Low for a further 1 hour.

6   Serve with crusty bread.

freezing tip
• Make and purée the soup without adding the milk or prawns, then cool and freeze the soup in a rigid container. Stir in the milk and prawns when reheating.

cream of chicken soup

4-6   **10** MINS   **6-10** hrs LOW   **Chunks of white bread**

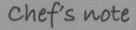

Chef's note

Cream of chicken is a soup that is popular in most families, from the youngest member to grandparents. This home-made version is delicious yet so easy to make and far surpasses any canned version. Tarragon is an excellent herb to flavour chicken.

15 ml/1 tbsp **oil**

225 g/8 oz **chicken**, diced

1 **onion**, chopped

25 g/1 oz **pearl barley**

5 ml/1 tsp **chopped fresh tarragon**

1 litre/1¾ pts/4¼ cups **chicken stock**

Salt and freshly ground black pepper

300 ml/½ pt/1¼ cups **double (heavy) cream**

1   Preheat the slow cooker on High.

2   Heat the oil in a frying pan and fry the chicken until opaque and the onion until soft. Transfer to the slow cooker and add all the remaining ingredients except the cream.

3   Cook on Low for 6–10 hours.

4   Purée the soup, then stir in the cream and reheat gently without allowing the soup to boil.

5   Serve with chunks of white bread.

freezing tip

• Make and purée the soup without adding the cream, then cool and freeze the soup in a rigid container. Stir in the cream when reheating.

curried apple soup

Chef's note

Apple and curry is a very successful flavour combination, and the lemon zest and juice imparts a refreshing tartness. Try making this soup in the autumn when apples are at their best and most plentiful.

6

15 MINS

6-8 hrs LOW

Wholemeal rolls

25 g/1 oz/2 tbsp **butter or margarine**

1 **onion**, finely chopped

10–15 ml/2–3 tsp **curry powder**

30 ml/2 tbsp **plain (all-purpose) flour**

1 litre/1¾ pts/4¼ cups **chicken stock**

Grated zest and juice of ½ **lemon**

700 g/1½ lb **cooking (tart) apples**, peeled, cored and chopped

Salt and freshly ground black pepper

150 ml/¼ pt/⅔ cup **soured (dairy sour) cream** or **plain yoghurt**

1 Preheat the slow cooker on High.

2 Heat the butter or margarine in a frying pan and fry the onion until transparent.

3 Stir in the curry powder and flour, then gradually add the stock, lemon zest and juice and apples. Season well with salt and pepper. Bring to the boil, then transfer to the slow cooker.

4 Cook on Low for 6–8 hours.

5 Purée the soup, then reheat and stir in the cream or yoghurt.

6 Serve with wholemeal rolls.

freezing tip

• Make and purée the soup without adding the cream or yoghurt, then cool and freeze the soup in a rigid container. Stir in the cream or yoghurt when reheating.

cucumber & mint soup

  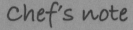 

6 | **10 MINS** | **4-8 hrs LOW** | **Bread sticks**

Chef's note

An elegant chilled soup that takes full advantage of the refreshing combination of cucumber and mint. What could be more cooling on a hot summer's day?

25 g/1 oz/2 tbsp **butter or margarine**

1 **onion**, chopped

1 large **cucumber**, peeled and sliced

600 ml/1 pt/2½ cups **chicken or vegetable stock**

30 ml/2 tbsp **chopped fresh mint leaves**

Salt and freshly ground black pepper

300 ml/½ pt/1¼ cups **milk**

90 ml/6 tbsp **plain yoghurt** or **crème fraîche**

1   Preheat the slow cooker on High.

2   Heat the butter or margarine in a frying pan and fry the onion until transparent.

3   Stir in the cucumber, stock, mint and salt and pepper and bring to the boil. Transfer to the slow cooker.

4   Cook on Low for 4–8 hours.

5   Purée the soup and stir in the milk.

6   Allow to cool, then chill until ready to serve in chilled bowls with 15 ml/1 tbsp yoghurt or crème fraîche swirled into each bowl.

7   Serve with bread sticks.

serving tip

• This soup can also be served hot with crisp bread croûtons.

freezing tip

• To freeze, make and purée the soup without adding the milk, then cool and freeze the soup in a rigid container. Stir in the milk when serving.

vichyssoise

6

10 MINS

8-10hrs LOW

Chef's note

Culinary historians are divided on the origins of vichyssoise; some say it was first created in France, others that it is an American invention. Wherever the truth lies, this classic chilled soup now has almost 'retro' status – but is no less delicious for that!

50 g/2 oz/¼ cup **unsalted (sweet) butter**

2 **onions**, chopped

1 **garlic clove**, crushed

700 g/1½ lb **leeks**, thinly sliced

2 **potatoes**, chopped

900 ml/1½ pts/3¾ cups **chicken stock**

Salt and freshly ground black pepper

90 ml/6 tbsp **double (heavy) cream**

Snipped fresh chives

1   Preheat the slow cooker on High.

2   Heat the butter in a frying pan and fry the onions, garlic and leeks gently for 3–4 minutes.

3   Add the potatoes and stock, season with salt and pepper and bring to the boil, then transfer to the slow cooker.

4   Cook on Low for 8–10 hours.

5   Purée the soup or rub through a sieve (strainer).

6   Allow to cool, then chill until ready to serve garnished with a swirl of cream and sprinkled with chives.

freezing tip

• Make the soup without adding the garlic, then cool and freeze the soup in a rigid container. Season with crushed garlic or garlic salt when ready to serve and garnish with the cream and chives.

mulligatawny soup

4-6 **15** MINS **4-5** hrs HIGH Granary bread

Chef's note

The name 'mulligatawny' comes from the Tamil *millagu* (pepper) and thanni (water), though the heat in this 'pepper water' comes from the curry powder spices as well as pepper itself. It is an Anglo-Indian creation that is also very popular in Sri Lanka.

50 g/2 oz/¼ cup **butter or margarine**

1 **cooking (tart) apple**, peeled and sliced

1 **onion**, sliced

1 **carrot**, sliced

30 ml/2 tbsp **curry powder**

45 ml/3 tbsp **plain (all-purpose) flour**

1 litre/1¾ pts/4¼ cups **chicken or vegetable stock**

2 **chicken portions**, skinned

A few drops of lemon juice

Salt and freshly ground black pepper

1   Preheat the slow cooker on High.

2   Heat the butter or margarine in a frying pan and fry the apple, onion and carrot for 2–3 minutes. Stir in the curry powder and flour and fry for 1 minute.

3   Stir in the stock and bring to the boil, then transfer to the slow cooker and add the chicken portions.

4   Cook on High for 4–5 hours.

5   Remove the chicken portions and slice the meat.

6   Purée the vegetables and stock, then return the chicken. Season with lemon juice, salt and pepper and serve.

7   Serve with granary bread.

starters & snacks

The gentle heat of the slow cooker is perfect f
cooking pâtés, making them firm with a smooth textu
and a delicate blend of flavours. They freeze well to
and are best if cut into individual servings an
interleaved with foil or greaseproof (waxed) paper an
over-wrapped with foil before freezing. Simply defro
at room temperature and they will be ready to serve

You'll find you can make all kinds of things in a slo
cooker that you wouldn't expect, such as the delicio
vegetable and cheese omelette in this section.

starters & snacks

Starters and snacks tips

- All these recipes can be teamed with salad and crusty bread to make a light lunch or supper.

- Use the slow cooker for your starter when you are entertaining if you know you will be using all your burners for the main course.

- Many of the recipes in the Vegetables section would also make good starters if served in smaller portions.

- Bags of salad leaves make an easy accompaniment to a light lunch.

eggs florentine

Chef's note

Eggs florentine is a dish often served for breakfast when cooked conventionally but when made in the slow cooker it can also be a wonderful starter before a lighter main course, or a very special supper for when you had a main meal earlier in the day.

4

15 MINS

3 hrs HIGH

25 g/1 oz/2 tbsp **butter or margarine**

450 g/1 lb **spinach**, roughly chopped

4 **eggs**

For the white sauce

25 g/1 oz/2 tbsp **butter or margarine**

25 g/1 oz/¼ cup **plain (all-purpose) flour**

300 ml/½ pt/1¼ cups **milk**

Salt and freshly ground black pepper

75 g/3 oz/¾ cup **cheese**, finely grated

1   Butter the inside of the slow cooker and preheat on High.

2   Arrange the spinach in the slow cooker and cook on High for 1 hour.

3   To make the white sauce, heat the butter or margarine in a pan and stir in the flour. Cook gently for 2–3 minutes, stirring continuously.

4   Gradually add the milk, still stirring, and bring to the boil. Season well with salt and pepper.

5   Use the base of a cup to make four 'wells' in the spinach. Break one egg into each, then pour the prepared sauce over.

6   Cook on High for a further 2 hours.

7   Serve sprinkled with the grated cheese.

avocado with crab

4-6 **15** MINS **2-3** hrs LOW A green salad

Chef's note

A really mouth-watering starter and one that is guaranteed to impress. You should use avocadoes that are at just the right stage or ripeness, when they yield to gentle pressure when squeezed in the palm of the hand. The fruit will ripen quicker in a brown paper bag, especially if you put an apple in as well.

2 **avocados**

Salt

Lemon juice

15 g/½ oz/1 tbsp **butter or margarine**

15 ml/1 tbsp **plain (all-purpose) flour**

150 ml/¼ pt/⅔ cup **milk**

3 **tomatoes**, skinned, quartered and sliced

30 ml/2 tbsp **tomato purée** (paste)

100 g/4 oz/1 small can of **crab meat**, drained

A pinch of **grated nutmeg**

150 ml/¼ pt/⅔ cup **water**

1 Preheat the slow cooker on High.

2 Halve and stone (pit) the avocados and sprinkle with salt and lemon juice to prevent discoloration.

3 Melt the butter or margarine, stir in the flour and cook for 1 minute, stirring. Whisk in the milk, then bring to the boil, stirring continuously, and cook until thickened.

4 Stir in the tomatoes, tomato purée, crab meat and nutmeg.

5 Spoon the crab mixture into the hollows of the avocado halves and arrange in the slow cooker. Pour the water around them.

6 Cook on Low for 2–3 hours.

7 Serve with a green salad.

chicken liver pâté

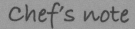

8 **20 MINS** **5-7 hrs HIGH** **Melba toast or crusty bread**

4 **streaky bacon** rashers (slices), rinded

450 g/1 lb **chicken livers**

1 **onion**, sliced

2 **whole cloves**

2 **bay leaves**

1 **bouquet garni** sachet

30 ml/2 tbsp **water**

Salt and freshly ground black pepper

50 g/2 oz/¼ cup **butter or margarine**

50 g/2 oz/½ cup **plain (all-purpose) flour**

150 ml/¼ pt/⅔ cup **milk**

1 **garlic clove**, crushed

30 ml/2 tbsp **double (heavy) cream**

1 **egg**

1   Preheat the slow cooker on High.

2   Stretch the bacon slices with the back of a knife, then lay them across the base of an ovenproof pâté dish.

3   Put the livers, onion, cloves, bay leaves, bouquet garni and a pinch of salt in a pan and just cover with water. Bring to the boil, then simmer for a few minutes until the livers stiffen. Leave to cool.

4   Discard the cloves, bay leaves and bouquet garni. Put the liver, onion and water in a food processor and purée until smooth.

5   Heat the butter or margarine in a pan, stir in the flour and cook for 1 minute. Gradually stir in the milk, then bring to the boil and simmer for 2 minutes, stirring continuously. Add the liver, garlic, cream and egg and season with salt and pepper. Transfer to the prepared dish, cover with foil and place in the slow cooker. Surround with sufficient boiling water to come almost to the top of the dish.

6   Cook on High for 5–7 hours.

7   Allow to cool, then chill before slicing.

8   Serve with melba toast or crusty bread.

freezing tip
• Pâté is best frozen in slices interleaved with greaseproof (waxed) paper.

chicken & lamb pâté

8 | **20** MINS | **3-4** hrs HIGH | Crusty bread

Chef's note

You are unlikely to find any shop-bought pâté that uses both chicken and lambs' livers, though the combination is wonderful. This recipe makes a large quantity of pâté, so it is ideal for larger dinner parties or as part of a buffet when you are entertaining a crowd!

25 g/1 oz/2 tbsp **butter or margarine**

4 **streaky bacon** rashers (slices), rinded

1 **onion**, finely chopped

225 g/8 oz **chicken livers**

225 g/8 oz **lambs' liver**

225 g/8 oz **belly pork**, minced (ground)

1 **garlic clove**, crushed

1 **egg**, beaten

30 ml/2 tbsp **double (heavy) cream**

5 ml/1 tsp **mustard powder**

5 ml/1 tsp **dried sage**

Salt and freshly ground black pepper

1   Preheat the slow cooker on High.

2   Grease a 15 cm/6 in cake tin (pan) with a little of the butter or margarine. Stretch the bacon rashers by running them over the blunt edge of a knife, then line the prepared tin with the bacon, leaving the edges hanging over the sides.

3   Melt the remaining butter or margarine in a frying pan and fry the onion until transparent.

4   Add the chicken and lambs' livers and fry for 1 minute until sealed.

5   Mince (grind) the mixture, then mix with all the remaining ingredients and spoon into the prepared container. Press down lightly, fold the ends of the bacon over the top and cover with foil.

6   Place in the slow cooker and surround with sufficient boiling water to come half-way up the tin. Cook on High for 3–4 hours.

7   Remove the tin from the slow cooker and place a weight on the top while the pâté cools.

8   Serve with crusty bread.

freezing tip
• Pâté is best frozen in slices interleaved with greaseproof (waxed) paper.

vegetable & ham omelette

Chef's note

In this recipe, alternate layers of hash browns and ham, onions, peppers and cheese are topped with an omelette mixture to make an easy starter or a satisfying supper when served with bread and a salad.

4

20 MINS

4-5 hrs LOW

Bread and salad

225 g/8 oz frozen **shredded hash brown potatoes**

200 g/5 oz **cooked ham**, diced

1 small **onion**, diced

1 small **green (bell) pepper**, seeded and diced

75 g/3 oz **Cheddar cheese**, grated

4 **eggs**

75 ml/5 tbsp **milk**

Salt and freshly ground black pepper

1   Preheat the slow cooker on High.

2   Lightly grease the slow cooker. Place a third of the hash brown potatoes in a layer on the bottom, then add a layer of a third of the ham, onion, green pepper and cheese. Repeat the layers twice more.

3   Whisk together the eggs and milk and season with salt and pepper. Pour the mixture over the ingredients in the slow cooker.

4   Cook on Low for 4–5 hours.

5   Serve cut into wedges with bread and a salad.

chorizo & peppers

4 **15 MINS** **6 hrs LOW** **Mashed potatoes**

Chef's note

This Spanish-style mixture of chorizo, sweet onion and peppers makes a superbly moist sandwich filling. Or if that's just a little too messy for your liking, try it spooned over mashed potatoes or plain boiled rice.

400 g/14 oz **chorizo sausage**, casings removed and crumbled

1 **green (bell) pepper**, seeded and chopped

1 **sweet onion**, peeled and chopped

75 g/3 oz **tomato purée** (paste)

120 ml/4 fl oz/½ cup **red wine**

120 ml/4 fl oz/½ cup **water**

1 **garlic clove**, crushed

1   Preheat the slow cooker on High.

2   Place all the ingredients in a bowl. Stir until everything is evenly distributed, then transfer the mixture to the slow cooker.

3   Cook on Low for 4 hours.

4   Uncover the pot and cook an additional 2 hours to allow some of the liquid to evaporate.

5   Serve hot or cold with mashed potatoes.

seafood

Fish and seafood cooked in the slow cooker reta
every bit of delicate flavour and also remain beautiful
whole. The moist heat is so gentle that whole fish or fis
pieces do not disintegrate during cooking.

Slow cooking takes away the exact timing normal
necessary for fish cookery, although it does cook mo:
quickly than, say, meat or soup.

Because fish should be appreciated at its freshest,
think it should be eaten as soon as it is cooked, so I c
not think it is a good idea to freeze any of these recipe
Always thaw frozen fish completely before using in ar
of these recipes.

seafood tips

- Clean and trim fish in the usual way before cooking.

- Do not put too many whole fish in a slow cooker or the weight of the top ones could affect the finished appearance and texture of those at the bottom. Four is an ideal number.

- You can use stock, water, wine, cider or fruit juice to cook fish. You will need only small quantities to retain the best fish flavour.

- Thickening agents such as flour or cornflour (cornstarch) should be added to casserole-type dishes before slow cooking (see page 12). Where there is a sauce made from the cooking liquor to accompany the fish, you may prefer to thicken the sauce in a pan after cooking, while keeping the cooked fish warm.

- Cream, milk and egg yolks should be added to the slow cooker during the last 30 minutes of cooking.

- When adapting your own fish recipes, compare them with the recipes in this chapter. You will probably need less liquid in which to cook the dishes.

baked mackere & cod

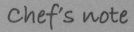

Chef's note

We should all eat more fish for a healthy diet, especially omega-rich oily fish, and mackerel is a really economical buy. In this recipe the richness of mackerel combines beautifully with the mellower flavour of cod, both complemented by the tomatoes.

 **4**

 **15 MINS**

 **2-4 hrs LOW**

 **New potatoes and peas**

25 g/1 oz/2 tbsp **butter or margarine**

1 **onion**, finely chopped

450 g/1 lb **mackerel fillets**, skinned and cubed

450 g/1 lb **cod fillets**, skinned and cubed

100 g/4 oz **button mushrooms**, sliced

225 g/8 oz **tomatoes**, skinned and sliced

Juice of 1 **lemon**

45 ml/3 tbsp **water**

Salt and freshly ground black pepper

Fried (sautéed) bread triangle to garnish

1   Preheat the slow cooker on High.

2   Heat the butter or margarine in a frying pan and fry the onion gently until transparent.

3   Stir in the remaining ingredients and bring to the boil, then transfer to the slow cooker.

4   Cook on Low for 2–4 hours.

5   Garnish with triangles of fried bread and serve with new potatoes and peas.

haddock casserole

4

10 MINS

3-6 hrs LOW

Boiled rice

Chef's note

This is a stylish dish that would be ideal for a dinner party, perhaps served with baby new potatoes and seasonal green vegetables. You can substitute other white fish for the haddock – but not smoked fish, which would overpower the delicate flavour of the courgettes.

700 g/1½ lb **haddock**, skinned and cubed

15 ml/1 tbsp **cornflour** (cornstarch)

15 ml/1 tbsp **oil**

1 **onion**, finely chopped

1 **garlic clove**, crushed

225 g/8 oz **courgettes (zucchini)**, thinly sliced

300 ml/½ pt/1¼ cups **dry white wine** or **cider**

1 **bay leaf**

1 **bouquet garni** sachet

1   Preheat the slow cooker on High.

2   Toss the fish with the cornflour until it is well covered, shaking off any excess.

3   Heat the oil in a frying pan and fry the onion, garlic and courgettes gently for 4–5 minutes.

4   Add the wine or cider, bay leaf and bouquet garni, then stir in the fish. Bring to the boil, then transfer to the slow cooker.

5   Cook on Low for 3–6 hours.

6   Discard the bay leaf and bouquet garni before serving with boiled rice.

eggs with smoked haddoc

4 | **5** MINS | **3** hrs LOW

Chef's note

Smoked haddock and eggs go so well together, and in the slow cooker they will bake together perfectly with no risk of either ingredient overcooking. Serve with your favourite accompaniments for a main course, or just with buttered bread for a supper dish.

25 g/1 oz/2 tbsp **butter or margarine**

700 g/1½ lb **smoked haddock**, in four equal pieces

90 ml/6 tbsp **milk**

90 ml/6 tbsp **water**

Freshly ground black pepper

4 **eggs**

1   Butter the inside of the slow cooker and preheat on High.

2   Arrange the haddock pieces in the slow cooker and pour over just enough of the milk and water to cover. Season with pepper.

3   Cook on Low for 2 hours.

4   Crack the eggs over the fish and continue to cook on Low for a further 1 hour.

5   Serve immediately.

cook's tip
• You could also use smoked mackerel for this dish.

herring with gooseberries

4-6

10 MINS

2-3 hrs LOW

New potatoes and salad

Chef's note

Herring are very high in healthy omega-3 fatty acids and have been a staple food source since 3000 BC; at one time this fish was known as 'two-eyed steak'! Gooseberries and herrings are a traditional British combination – the unique flavour of the fruit complements the fish perfectly.

15 g/½ oz/1 tbsp **butter or margarine**

450 g/1 lb **boned herrings**

Salt and freshly ground black pepper

225 g/8 oz **gooseberries**, trimmed

30 ml/2 tbsp **caster (superfine) sugar**

75 ml/5 tbsp **water**

1   Butter the base of the slow cooker and preheat on High.

2   Season the inside of the herrings with salt and pepper.

3   Arrange the gooseberries in the slow cooker, sprinkle with the sugar and pour on the water. Lay the seasoned herrings on top.

4   Cook on Low for 2–3 hours.

5   Serve with new potatoes and salad.

cook's tip
• This is also ideal for mackerel.

cod in tomato sauce

4

5 MINS

3-5 hrs LOW

Fresh green vegetables

Chef's note

If you think that cod can be a rather bland fish, needing complicated sauces using exotic ingredients to make it interesting, think again! This dish is so simple and delicious, even though it uses just canned tomatoes and tomato purée. You can also cook it for 2–3 hours on High, if you want a speedier meal.

150 g/6 oz **cod fillets**

15 ml/1 tbsp **tomato purée (paste)**

14 oz/400 g/1 large can of **peeled plum tomatoes**, chopped

Garlic salt to taste

Freshly ground black pepper

1 **green (bell) pepper**, diced

1   Preheat the slow cooker on Low.

2   Stir the tomato purée into the chopped tomatoes in a bowl, season to taste with garlic salt and pepper and add the green pepper.

3   Lay the fish fillets in the slow cooker and pour the tomato mixture over.

4   Cook on Low for 3–5 hours.

5   Serve with fresh green vegetables, such as broccoli or green beans.

cook's tip
• You can use any firm-fleshed white fish for this recipe.

rollmop herrings

4

10 MINS

4-6 hrs LOW

Salad and boiled potatoes

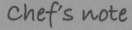

Chef's note

These rollmops can be served hot from the slow cooker with salad and boiled potatoes for a main meal, or left to cool to eat as a starter. Small boned mackerel or pilchards can be cooked in the same way.

6–8 **herrings**

Salt and freshly ground black pepper

150 ml/¼ pt/⅔ cup **malt vinegar**

150 ml/¼ pt/⅔ cup **water**

3 **shallots**, thinly sliced

2 **bay leaves**

1 **blade of mace**

6 **whole black peppercorns**

1 Preheat the slow cooker on High.

2 Scale, clean and bone the herrings and discard the heads and tails. Season lightly with salt and pepper. Roll up from the tail end, skin-side out, and arrange in the slow cooker.

3 Mix together the remaining ingredients in a saucepan and season with salt and pepper. Bring to the boil, then pour over the herrings.

4 Cook on Low for 4–6 hours.

5 Arrange the herrings in a serving dish and pour the cooking liquor over.

6 Serve with salad and boiled potatoes

storing tip
• Rollmop herrings keep very well in the fridge.

seafood jambalaya

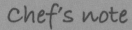

4 · **10** MINS · **5-6** hrs LOW · Green salad

Chef's note

The slow cooker is great for this mixed seafood recipe – it practically cooks itself! Precooking the rice gives an even better finished dish because rice has a tendency to 'blow' and become sticky if it's cooked too long.

1 **onion**, peeled and chopped

1 **green (bell) pepper**, cored, seeded and chopped

1 **garlic clove**, peeled and crushed

8 oz/225 g) sliced of **gammon ham**, diced

14 oz/400 g/1 large can of **peeled plum tomatoes**, chopped

15 ml/1 tbsp **tomato purée (paste)**

2.5 ml/1/2 tsp **chilli powder**

15 ml/1 tbsp **chopped fresh basil**

150 ml/¼ pt/⅔ cup **chicken or fish stock**

4 oz/100 g **cooked chicken**, diced

450 g/1 lb **cooked, peeled prawns (shrimp)**, thawed if frozen

450 g/1 lb/4 cups **cooked rice**

Chopped fresh parsley to garnish

1 Preheat the slow cooker on High.

2 Put all the ingredients except the chicken, prawns and rice in the slow cooker, stir thoroughly and cook on Low for 4–5 hours.

3 Stir in the chicken, prawns and rice and cook a further 45 minutes on High.

4 Garnish with freshly chopped parsley and serve with a green salad.

cook's tip

- If you want to cook the rice in the slow cooker from raw, easy-cook rice gives the best results. Add it uncooked to this mixed seafood recipe 2 hours before serving.

stuffed plaice with orange

4 | **10** MINS | **2-3** hrs LOW | A salad or vegetables

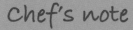

Chef's note

Another recipe that takes full advantage of the natural affinity of eggs and fish, and adds the citrus zing of fresh orange juice. Serve with just a simple dressed salad for a light meal, or with new potatoes and a green vegetable for dinner or supper.

50 g/2 oz/¼ cup **butter or margarine**

100 g/4 oz **mushrooms**, chopped

2 **hard-boiled (hard-cooked) eggs**, chopped

Salt and freshly ground black pepper

8 small **plaice fillets**, skinned

Juice of 2 **oranges**

1 Preheat the slow cooker on High.

2 Heat 15 g/½ oz/1 tbsp of the butter or margarine in a saucepan and fry the mushrooms gently for 1–2 minutes.

3 Stir in the eggs and season with salt and pepper.

4 Place a little of the mixture on the skinned side of each fillet. Roll up and secure with cocktail sticks (toothpicks).

5 Arrange the fish in the slow cooker and dot with the remaining butter or margarine. Pour the orange juice over.

6 Cook on Low for 2½–3 hours.

7 Serve with salad or vegetables.

italian-style mullet

4

10 MINS

2-3 hrs HIGH

Rice and salad

25 g/1 oz/2 tbsp **butter or margarine**

2 **tomatoes**, skinned and sliced

1 **green (bell) pepper**, seeded and sliced

100 g/4 oz **mushrooms**, sliced

Salt and freshly ground black pepper

4 **red mullet**, scaled and trimmed

60 ml/4 tbsp **red wine**

15 ml/1 tbsp **snipped fresh chives**

1   Grease the slow cooker with a little of the butter or margarine and preheat on High.

2   Arrange the tomato, pepper and mushroom slices in the slow cooker and season with salt and pepper.

3   Place the fish on top of the vegetables and season with salt and pepper. Pour the wine over and dot with the remaining butter or margarine. Sprinkle with the chives.

4   Cook on High for 2–3 hours.

5   Serve with rice and salad.

salmon poached in wine

4

5 MINS

3 hrs LOW

New potatoes and salad

Oil for greasing

1 kg/2¼ lb **salmon piece**

300 ml/½ pt/1¼ cups **white wine**

1 **bay leaf**

A **sprig of parsley**

1.5 ml/¼ tsp **salt**

Black pepper

Grated zest and juice of 1 **lemon**

Chef's note

You should be able to fit in the salmon in the slow cooker in one piece, but if you have a smaller model you can cut it in half and arrange the pieces on the bottom of the crock pot. Serve either hot or cold – it is delicious cold with a salad and brown bread and butter.

1   Brush the inside of the slow cooker with oil.

2   Rinse and dry the salmon piece, then place it in the slow cooker.

3   Add the wine, bay leaf, parsley, salt, a grinding of pepper and the lemon zest and juice.

4   Cook on Low for about 3 hours.

5   Serve with new potatoes and salad.

creamy fish pie with potato

4　　**15 MINS**　　**2-3 hrs HIGH**　　Broccoli

Chef's note

Fish pie is a traditional British dish and a perennial family favourite. This recipe suggests using cod fillets but you could substitute other white fish such as haddock or halibut for a change, or a mixture.

450 g/1 lb **cod fillets**, skinned and cut into chunks

1 **onion**, chopped

1 **garlic clove**, crushed

100 g/4 oz **button mushrooms**, sliced

3 **sprigs of parsley**

1 **bay leaf**

Salt and freshly ground black pepper

150 ml/¼ pt/⅔ cup **fish or vegetable stock**

25 g/1 oz/2 tbsp **butter or margarine**

30 ml/2 tbsp **plain (all-purpose) flour**

250 ml/8 fl oz/1 cup **milk**

1 **hard-boiled (hard-cooked) egg**, sliced

15 ml/1 tbsp **chopped fresh parsley**

700 g/1½ lb **potatoes**, cooked and mashed

1   Preheat the slow cooker on High.

2   Arrange the fish, onion, garlic and mushrooms in the slow cooker. Add the parsley sprigs and bay leaf and season with salt and pepper. Pour the stock over and stir gently.

3   Cook on High for 2–3 hours.

4   Strain the liquid and reserve 150 ml/¼ pt/⅔ cup.

5   Melt the butter or margarine in a saucepan, stir in the flour and cook gently for 1 minute. Whisk in the milk and the reserved liquid, then bring to the boil and simmer for 2 minutes, stirring. Season with salt and pepper.

6   Pour the sauce over the fish, add the eggs and stir gently.

7   Mix the parsley into the cooked potatoes and spread over the top of the dish. Brown in a preheated oven at 200°C/400°F/gas mark 6/fan oven 180°C or under a hot grill (broiler).

8   Serve with broccoli or another green vegetable.

trout in wine & lemon

4

5 MINS

3-4 hrs LOW

New potatoes and vegetables

Oil for greasing

4 **trout**, gutted and heads removed

4 oz/100 g **mushrooms**, sliced

150 ml/¼ pt/⅔ cup **white wine**

Grated zest and juice of 1 **lemon**

Freshly ground black pepper

1.5 ml/¼ tsp **salt**

150 ml/¼ pt/⅔ cup **double (heavy) cream, crème fraîche or soured (dairy sour) cream**

Chef's note

Trout is extremely tasty and healthy – it is low in calories and has a third of the fat of salmon and its valuable natural oils help to keep the skin and hair in good condition. This recipe would be lovely served with some new potatoes and lightly steamed green beans and cauliflower.

1   Grease the slow cooker with a little oil and place the trout tail to head in the bottom of the crock pot.

2   Add the mushrooms, wine, lemon zest and juice, a grinding of black pepper and the salt.

3   Cook on Low for 3–4 hours.

4   Stir in the cream, crème fraîche or soured cream and heat for a further 15 minutes or so.

5   Serve with new potatoes and vegetables.

prawn risotto

4 | 15 MINS | 3-4 hrs LOW | Green salad

15 ml/1 tbsp **oil**

2 **onions**, finely chopped

900 ml/1½ pts/3¾ cups **chicken stock**

225 g/8 oz **button mushrooms**, sliced

1 **green (bell) pepper**, seeded and chopped

2 **tomatoes**, skinned and sliced

165 g/6 oz/¼ cup **easy-cook long-grain rice**

225 g/8 oz cooked, **peeled prawns (shrimp)**

Salt and freshly ground black pepper

1 Preheat the slow cooker on High.

2 Heat the oil in a frying pan and fry the onions gently until transparent.

3 Add the stock, mushrooms and pepper and bring to the boil, then transfer to the slow cooker.

4 Stir in the tomatoes, rice and prawns.

5 Cook on Low for 3–4 hours.

6 Stir well, taste and adjust the seasoning, then serve at once with a green salad.

jamaican-style fish

4   **15** MINS   **4** hrs LOW   Rice and peas

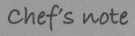

Chef's note

Serve this tasty tropical fish dish with rice and peas or perhaps boiled sweet potato. You may be able to fit the fish into the slow cooker whole, but if your model is a smaller one then cut them to fit.

Oil for frying

1 kg/2¼ lb **basa** or **snapper**

50 g/2 oz **butter**

1 **onion**, peeled and chopped

15 ml/1 tbsp **plain (all-purpose) flour**

30 ml/2 tbsp **soy sauce**

450 ml/¾ pt/2 cups **fish stock or water or a mix of water and white wine**

30 ml/2 tbsp **tomato purée (paste)**

2 **sprigs of thyme** or 5 ml/1 tsp **dried thyme**

Salt and freshly ground black pepper

1   Heat the slow cooker on Low.

2   Heat a little oil in a frying pan and fry the fish to seal. Place it in the slow cooker.

3   Melt the butter in the same pan and fry the onion until soft, then add the flour and mix to a roux.

4   Slowly stir in the soy sauce and cook for a couple of minutes, stirring all the time.

5   Stir in the stock, add the tomato purée and thyme and season to taste. Pour the sauce over the fish and cook on Low for 4 hours.

6   Serve with rice and peas.

meat

The slow cooker could almost have been designe specifically for cooking meat, both joints ar casseroles. The recipes can be left to cook all day (ar part of the evening too, if necessary) with no risk burning or overcooking, and without the worry checking, basting, turning or stirring. The slow, gent heat action tenderises even the toughest cuts of me and cooked joints will shrink much less than whe cooked conventionally.

Use the slow cooker to prepare exotic, delicate recip suitable for entertaining as well as for tasty casserole stews and roasts for every day. Whenever possible, u the juices that surround the meat as a rich sauce complete the meal.

The majority of slow cooked meat recipes can l frozen successfully. Any specific tips you need can l found at the end of the recipes. Always defrost froze meat completely before slow cooking. Remembe though, that partially frozen meat is easy to hand when chopping or slicing.

Meat tips

- Trim excess fat from the meat before cooking.

- Lightly browning the meat before slow cooking improves the flavour and appearance of joints and casseroles.

- Vegetables take longer to cook than meat so make sure they are diced small and immersed in the cooking liquid.

- Reduce the quantity of liquid by about half if you are adapting your own conventional recipes. If necessary, you can adjust the quantity of liquid before serving.

- Liquids for slow cooking meat can be water, stock, wine, cider, beer or fruit juice.

- If you are thickening a casserole, do so before cooking or for the final 1–1½ hours (see page 12), or thicken the cooking juices separately in a pan after you have cooked the meat.

- Add cream, milk or egg yolks during the final 30 minutes of cooking time.

- Cooking times for joints vary according to size, shape, quality, the proportion of meat to fat and bone, and personal taste. However, these guidelines should be helpful: cook a 1.25–1.5 kg (2½–3 lb) joint on High for 3–6 hours (3–5 hours for pork); cook a 1.6–2.25 kg (3½–5 lb) joint on High for 5–8 hours (4–6 hours for pork).

- To obtain a crisp skin for pork, do not fry the joint before slow cooking. Instead, finish the cooked joint under a hot grill (broiler) for about 10 minutes.

hungarian beef goulash

6

10 MINS

7-10 hrs LOW

Mashed potatoes

Chef's note

Goulash originated in Hungary and is a stew usually made of beef, onions, vegetables and – the essential ingredient – ground paprika. The name comes from the Hungarian word for a cattle stockman – *gulyás*.

45 ml/3 tbsp **plain (all-purpose) flour**

Salt and freshly ground black pepper

1 kg/2¼ lb **stewing steak**, cubed

45 ml/3 tbsp **oil**

3 **onions**, chopped

2 **green (bell) peppers**, seeded and sliced

300 ml/½ pt/1¼ cups **beef stock**

400 g/14 oz/1 large can of **chopped tomatoes**

45 ml/3 tbsp **tomato purée (paste)**

15 ml/1 tbsp **ground paprika**

1 **bouquet garni** sachet

Soured (dairy sour) cream or plain yoghurt to garnish

1 Preheat the slow cooker on High.

2 Season the flour with salt and pepper, then toss the meat in the flour, shaking off any excess.

3 Heat the oil in a frying pan and brown the meat lightly on all sides.

4 Stir in the onions and peppers and cook for 3 minutes.

5 Stir in the remaining ingredients and bring to the boil, then transfer to the slow cooker.

6 Cook on Low for 7–10 hours.

7 Discard the bouquet garni, adjust the seasoning to taste and stir well. Swirl in a spoonful of soured cream or yoghurt.

8 Serve with mashed potatoes.

freezing tip
• Freeze without the cream or yoghurt.

classic beef casserole

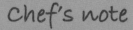

4

15 MINS

4-6 hrs LOW

Mashed potatoes and steamed vegetables

Chef's note

This is a filling recipe, full of flavour and perfect to leave in a slow cooker all day. You can use the cheaper cuts of beef as the long cooking will tenderise the meat and ensure the flavours are well mixed.

1 kg/450 g **chuck steak**, sliced as thinly as possible

45 ml/3 tbsp **plain (all-purpose) flour**

Salt and freshly ground black pepper

5 ml/1 tsp **dried mixed herbs**

Oil for frying

2 **bay leaves**

5 ml/1 tsbp **wholegrain mustard**

2.5 ml/½ tsp **chopped fresh thyme**

2.5 ml/½ tsp **chopped fresh rosemary**

2 **garlic cloves**, crushed

2 **large onions**, sliced

300 ml/½ pt/1¼ cups **beef stock**

1   Mix half the flour with some salt and pepper and the mixed herbs and use to coat the meat.

2   Heat a little oil in a frying pan and fry the meat over a medium heat until browned, then transfer to the slow cooker. Add the bay leaves, thyme and rosemary to the slow cooker.

3   Add a little more oil to the pan and fry the onions and garlic until softened and lightly browned. Remove from the heat and stir in the remaining flour and the mustard. Return to a low heat and add the stock slowly, stirring constantly, to make a smooth sauce.

4   Pour the sauce over the beef and herbs and add salt and pepper to taste.

5   Cook for 4–6 hours on Low.

6   Serve with mashed potatoes and steamed vegetables.

beef in red wine

6

15 MINS

7-10 hrs LOW

Carrots and celeriac

Chef's note

When cooking with wine, you certainly don't need to use the finest vintage Bordeaux – but don't think that a really cheap or inferior wine will 'do' as it will certainly adversely affect the flavour of the finished dish.

15 ml/1 tbsp **oil**

25 g/1 oz/2 tbsp **butter or margarine**

225 g/8 oz **streaky bacon**, rinded and chopped

2 **garlic cloves**, crushed

1 kg/2¼ lb **stewing steak**, cubed

30 ml/2 tbsp **plain (all-purpose) flour**

300 ml/½ pt/1¼ cups **red wine**

2 **bay leaves**

12 **small whole onions**

Salt and freshly ground black pepper

1   Preheat the slow cooker on High.

2   Heat the oil and butter in a frying pan and fry the bacon and garlic gently for 2–3 minutes.

3   Add the steak and stir over a low heat until lightly browned on all sides.

4   Stir in the flour, then slowly add the red wine, stirring until well blended. Add the bay leaves, onions and seasoning. Bring to the boil, then transfer to the slow cooker.

5   Cook on Low for 7–10 hours.

6   Discard the bay leaves and adjust the seasoning before serving.

7   Serve with carrots and celeriac.

freezing tip
• Cook without the garlic. Add crushed garlic or garlic salt when reheating.

classic pot roast

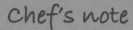   

8-10 **15 MINS** **6 hrs HIGH**

Chef's note

The quantities here will serve up to 10 people so it's the perfect trouble-free way to prepare well in advance for a party, leaving you to enjoy the evening with your guests. You will need a large slow cooker for this recipe.

1 **large onion**, diced

100 g/4 oz **baby carrots**, cut into ¼ in slices

1 **celery stick**, cut into 5 mm/¼ in slices

2 **garlic cloves**, chopped

1 **boneless beef joint**, about 1.5 kg/3 lb, tied

Olive oil

5 ml/1 tsp **salt**

1.5 ml/¼ tsp **freshly ground black pepper**

225 g/8 oz **button mushrooms**, sliced

4 sprigs of **fresh thyme**

1 **bay leaf**

250 ml/8 fl oz/1 cup **beef broth** (see page 22)

120 ml/4 fl oz/½ cup **dry red wine**

30 ml/2 tbsp **tomato purée (paste)**

45 ml/3 tbsp **plain (all-purpose) flour**

450 g/1 lb **egg noodles**

1   Layer the onion, carrots, celery and garlic in the slow cooker. Rub the joint all over with olive oil, then season the joint with the salt and pepper.

2   Scatter the mushrooms over the vegetables in the slow cooker and place the meat on top. Tuck the thyme sprigs and bay leaf into the mixture.

3   In medium-size bowl, whisk together the beef broth, wine and tomato purée. Pour over the meat.

4   Cook on High for 6 hours.

5   Remove the roast from the slow cooker and keep warm.

6   Pour the liquid with the vegetable mixture from the slow cooker into a medium-size saucepan, discarding the bay leaf and thyme sprigs. Bring to the boil.

7   Stir together 30 ml/2 tbsp of olive oil and the flour in a small cup until well blended and smooth. Stir the flour mixture into the liquid in the saucepan and boil, stirring, for about 1 minute until the liquid is slightly thickened.

8   Meanwhile, cook the noodles according to the packet directions, then drain thoroughly.

9   Slice the pot roast and serve with the gravy and noodles.

rich beef stroganoff

4

15 MINS

7-10 hrs LOW

Boiled potatoes

50 g/2 oz/¼ cup **butter** or **margarine**

2 **onions,** chopped

30 ml/2 tbsp **plain (all-purpose) flour**

Salt and freshly ground black pepper

700 g/1½ lb **braising steak**, cut into strips across the grain

300 ml/½ pt/1¼ cups **beef stock**

100 g/4 oz **mushrooms,** sliced

5 ml/1 tsp **dried mixed herbs**

15 ml/1 tbsp **tomato purée (paste)**

10 ml/2 tsp **French mustard**

150 ml/¼ pt/⅔ cup **single (light) cream**

15 ml/1 tbsp **chopped fresh parsley**

1 Preheat the slow cooker on High.

2 Heat the butter or margarine in a large frying pan and fry the onions gently until transparent.

3 Season the flour with salt and pepper, then toss the meat in the mixture, shaking off any excess.

4 Add the meat to the onions and stir until browned.

5 Stir in all the remaining ingredients except the cream and parsley and bring to the boil, then transfer to the slow cooker.

6 Cook on Low for 7–10 hours.

7 Just before serving, stir well, swirl the cream on top and garnish with the parsley.

8 Serve with boiled potatoes.

freezing tip

• Omit the cream and parsley before freezing. Stir the cream into the dish after reheating but do not allow the mixture to boil.

traditional irish stew

6 | **20 MINS** | **3.5 hrs LOW** | **Potatoes and carrots**

Chef's note

This is a traditional thick winter stew that is ideal for the slow cooker as you can vary the ingredients to take account of what's in season and what you have in the pantry, while the long, slow cooking makes for beautifully tender meat. It's a great advantage in using a slow cooker that you can choose the cheaper cuts of meat and cook them to perfection.

15 ml/1 tbsp **vegetable oil**

900 g/2 lb **stewing beef**, cubed

5 ml/1 tsp **dried sage**

6 **potatoes**, peeled and cubed

4 **carrots**, diced

100 g/4 oz **mushrooms**, sliced

1 **onion**, chopped

2.5 ml/½ tsp **celery seed**

5 ml/1 tsp **Worcestershire sauce**

450 ml/¾ pt/2 cups **beef stock**

Salt and freshly ground black pepper

10 ml/2 tsp **cornflour (cornstarch)**

1   Heat the oil in a frying pan over a medium-high heat. Add the beef and sage and fry until browned on all sides.

2   Drain off any fat and spoon the beef into the slow cooker.

3   Add the potatoes, carrots, mushrooms, onion and celery seed and mix together gently.

4   Add the Worcestershire sauce to the stock and pour over the ingredients so they are just covered. Season with salt and pepper.

5   Cover and cook on High for about 3 hours, stirring occasionally.

6   Blend the cornflour with a little water in a small bowl until smooth. Stir through the stew, then re-cover and allow to cook for 15–20 minutes until thickened.

7   Serve with potatoes and carrots.

herb-stuffed beef olives

 **4**

 **20 MINS**

 **6-9 hrs LOW**

 Mediterranean vegetables

Chef's note

Contrary to their name, these pieces of beef steak rolled around a stuffing do not usually contain olives! They are known as braciole or involtini in southern and northern Italy respectively. The filling can vary; here we use a tasty mixture of suet, breadcrumbs and herbs.

450 g/1 lb **braising steak**

30 ml/2 tbsp **oil**

1 **onion**, sliced

30 ml/2 tbsp **plain (all-purpose) flour**

450 ml/¾ pt/2 cups **beef stock**

For the stuffing

50 g/2 oz/1 cup **fresh breadcrumbs**

25 g/1 oz/2 tbsp **shredded suet**

2.5 ml/½ tsp **dried mixed herbs**

5 ml/1 tsp **chopped fresh parsley**

Salt and freshly ground black pepper

1 **egg**, beaten

5 ml/1 tsp **lemon juice**

1   Preheat the slow cooker on High.

2   Cut the steak into about eight thin slices across the grain, each about 10 cm/4 in square.

3   Mix together all the stuffing ingredients and spread a little on to each slice of steak. Roll up and secure with cocktail sticks (toothpicks).

4   Heat the oil in a frying pan and lightly brown the meat rolls. Remove from the pan.

5   In the same pan, fry the onion until transparent. Stir in the flour and cook until browned. Gradually stir in the stock and season to taste with salt and pepper. Bring to the boil, stirring well, then transfer to the slow cooker and arrange the meat on top.

6   Cook on Low for 6–9 hours.

7   Arrange the beef olives on a serving plate and remove the cocktail sticks. Keep warm.

8   Strain the gravy and reheat in a small pan if necessary. Pour over the meat just before serving with Mediterranean vegetables.

mexican beef stew

4

20 MINS

4-5 hrs LOW

Tortillas or cornbread

Chef's note

This hearty Mexican-style beef stew is excellent with tortillas or cornbread, and is also great as a burrito filling. It's a real meal for the lads for after the pub or a football match!

700 g/1¾ lb **braising steak**, cut into 1½ inch cubes

350 g/12 oz **potatoes**, unpeeled and diced

1 **small onion**, chopped

1 **red (bell) pepper**, cut into strips

2 **garlic cloves**, crushed

15 g/½ oz **plain (all-purpose) flour**

15 g/½ oz **chilli powder**

A pinch of **ground cumin**

2.5 ml/½ tsp **salt**

350 ml/12 fl oz/1⅓ cups **beef broth** (see page 22)

1   Preheat the slow cooker on High.

2   Combine the beef, potatoes, onion, peppers, and garlic in a large bowl.

3   In a small bowl, mix together the flour, chilli powder, cumin and salt. Toss the beef mixture with the flour mixture until evenly coated.

4   Place the mixture in the slow cooker and pour in enough beef broth to barely cover the meat. If you don't have quite enough, you can fill the rest of the way with water.

5   Cook on Low for 4–5 hours until the beef is tender.

6   Serve with tortillas or cornbread.

spaghetti bolognese

4

15 MINS

3-4 hrs HIGH

Green salad

Chef's note

Spaghetti Bolognese – and variations on it – are served up in so many households, and the dish is a particular favourite in student kitchens. For the busy family, though, this slow-cooked version is ideal and, to save time when you come home seriously hungry after a day out, you could use fresh spaghetti instead of dried, which takes only 5 minutes to cook.

30 ml/2 tbsp **oil**

1 **onion**, chopped

1 **carrot**, chopped

1 **celery stick**, chopped

2 **garlic cloves**, crushed

450 g/1 lb **minced (ground) beef**

50 g/2 oz **mushrooms**, chopped

400 g/14 oz/large can of **chopped tomatoes**

1 **bay leaf**

2.5 ml/½ tsp **dried oregano**

Salt and freshly ground black pepper

225 g/8 oz **spaghetti**

1   Preheat the slow cooker on High.

2   Heat the oil in a large frying pan and fry the onion, carrot, celery and garlic until transparent.

3   Add the meat and fry, stirring well, until it is browned and well broken up.

4   Stir in the mushrooms, tomatoes, bay leaf and oregano and season to taste with salt and pepper. Transfer to the slow cooker.

5   Cook on High for 3–4 hours.

6   When almost ready to serve, bring a large pan of salted water to the boil, add the spaghetti and boil for about 10 minutes until *al dente*. Drain well.

7   Remove the bay leaf from the Bolognese sauce and serve the sauce over the spaghetti with a green salad on the side.

beef lasagne

4

20 MINS

4-6 hrs LOW

Green salad

Chef's note

Making a lasagne from scratch in the conventional way can be rather fiddly and leave you with a kitchen full of steam by the time you put the dish in the oven. Using the slow cooker means that all the preparation is done well in advance so you can sit down and enjoy your meal just as much as everyone else at the table!

30 ml/2 tbsp **oil**

1 **onion**, chopped

1 **garlic clove**, chopped

1 **carrot**, chopped

1 **celery stick**, chopped

450 g/1 lb **minced (ground) beef**

50 g/2 oz **mushrooms**, chopped

15 ml/1 tbsp **plain (all-purpose) flour**

30 ml/2 tbsp **tomato purée (paste)**

15 ml/1 tbsp **chopped fresh flatleaf parsley**

Salt and freshly ground black pepper

300 ml/½ pt/1¼ cups **white sauce** (see pages 52–3)

175 g/6 oz **no-need-to-precook lasagne sheets**

50 g/2 oz/½ cup freshly grated **Parmesan cheese**

1   Preheat the slow cooker on High.

2   Heat the oil in a large frying pan and fry the onion, garlic, carrot and celery until transparent.

3   Stir in the beef and fry until well browned and broken up. Stir in the mushrooms.

4   Mix in the flour and cook until browned. Stir in the tomato purée and parsley and season with salt and pepper.

5   Make up the white sauce.

6   Layer the meat, lasagne sheets and white sauce into the slow cooker, finishing with a layer of lasagne, then white sauce. Sprinkle with half the Parmesan.

7   Cook on Low for 4–6 hours.

8   Sprinkle with the remaining Parmesan and serve with a green salad.

cook's tip

• Grating your own Parmesan – rather than buying ready-grated – will give you the best flavour.

chilli con carne

Chef's note

This popular dish is widely – and wrongly – believed to have its origins in Mexico. Wherever it was first created, it is now the official dish of Texas! We suggest serving it with tacos, though it is also delicious mopped up with rice.

4

10 MINS

6-8 hrs LOW

Tacos and a green salad

15 ml/1 tbsp **oil**

50 g/2 oz **streaky bacon**, rinded and chopped

1 **onion**, chopped

1 **green (bell) pepper**, seeded and chopped

2 **celery sticks**, chopped

450 g/1 lb **minced (ground) beef**

10 ml/2 tsp **chilli powder**

400 g/14 oz/large can of **red kidney beans**, drained and rinsed

400 g/14 oz/large can of **chopped tomatoes**

Salt and freshly ground black pepper

1. Preheat the slow cooker on High.

2. Heat the oil in a large frying pan and fry the bacon, onion, pepper and celery until transparent.

3. Stir in the beef and fry until lightly browned and well broken up.

4. Stir in the chilli powder, kidney beans and tomatoes and season with salt and pepper. Transfer to the slow cooker.

5. Cook on Low for 6–8 hours.

6. Check and adjust the seasoning before serving with tacos and a green salad.

beefburgers in tomato sauce

4 | **10** MINS | **4-6** hrs LOW | Chips and peas

450 g/1 lb **minced (ground) beef**

100 g/4 oz/2 cups **fresh breadcrumbs**

1 **small onion**, finely chopped

10 ml/2 tsp **dried mixed herbs**

Salt and freshly ground black pepper

25 g/1 oz/2 tbsp **butter or margarine**

1 **beef stock cube**

150 ml/¼ pt/⅔ cup **boiling water**

10 oz/275 g/medium can of **condensed cream of tomato soup**

1   Preheat the slow cooker on High.

2   Mix together the minced beef, breadcrumbs, onion, herbs and seasoning. Shape into eight burgers.

3   Heat the butter or margarine in a frying pan and brown the burgers quickly on both sides. Transfer to the slow cooker.

4   Dissolve the stock cube in the boiling water, then mix into the tomato soup. Pour into the frying pan, mix with the cooking juices from the burgers and bring to the boil. Pour the sauce over the burgers.

5   Cook on Low for 4–6 hours.

6   Serve with chips and peas.

freezing tip

• Arrange the burgers on a foil tray and pour the sauce over. Cover and freeze.

sausage & mushroom bake

Chef's note

Three ever-populars – sausages, mushrooms and baked beans – only this time not cooked on the hob and served up for breakfast but slow-cooked with sliced potatoes and tomato purée with just a dash of chilli for heat.

6 **10 MINS** **6-8 hrs LOW** **Mashed potatoes and cauliflower**

30 ml/2 tbsp **oil**

1 **onion**, chopped

450 g/1 lb **potatoes**, thinly sliced

450 g/1 lb **skinless beef sausages**, halved

450 g/1 lb/large can of **baked beans**

100 g/4 oz **button mushrooms,** halved

15 ml/1 tbsp **chilli powder**

15 ml/1 tbsp **tomato purée (paste)**

150 ml/¼ pt/⅔ cup **water**

Salt and freshly ground black pepper

1   Preheat the slow cooker on High.

2   Heat the oil in a large frying pan and fry the onion and potatoes gently for 5 minutes.

3   Add the remaining ingredients, season with salt and pepper and bring to the boil. Transfer to the slow cooker.

4   Cook on Low for 6–8 hours.

5   Serve with mashed potatoes and cauliflower.

lamb cutlets in red wine sauce

4

10 MINS

4-6 hrs LOW

Sauté potatoes and French beans

Lamb cutlets can be rather expensive but are undoubtedly a treat. All the more reason, then, to treat them to slow cooking so they are meltingly tender and retain all of their succulent flavour.

30 ml/2 tbsp **oil**

2 **onions**, thinly sliced into rings

8 **lamb cutlets**

Salt and freshly ground black pepper

15 ml/1 tbsp **cornflour (cornstarch)**

300 ml/½ pt/1¼ cups **red wine**

10 ml/2 tsp **dried rosemary**

1   Preheat the slow cooker on High.

2   Heat the oil in a frying pan and fry the onions gently until transparent. Transfer to the slow cooker.

3   Season the lamb cutlets with salt and pepper, then brown on all sides in the same pan. Arrange on top of the onions in the slow cooker.

4   Stir the cornflour into the remaining fat in the pan, then slowly add the red wine, stirring continuously. Add the rosemary. Bring to the boil, then pour the sauce over the cutlets.

5   Cook on Low for 4–6 hours.

6   Serve with sauté potatoes and French beans.

lamb in mushroom sauc

4-6

10 MINS

6-9 hrs LOW

Boiled potatoes a purple sprouting broccoli

Chef's note

This recipe takes so little time and trouble to prepare and the results are delicious, with tender meat and perfectly cooked vegetables. You can buy bags of ready-cubed frozen lamb at the supermarket but you will need to allow it to thaw before using.

15 ml/1 tbsp **oil**

25 g/1 oz/2 tbsp **butter or margarine**

2 **onions**, thinly sliced

1 **garlic clove**, crushed

1 **green (bell) pepper**, seeded and sliced

700 g/1¾ lb **lean lamb**, cubed

100 g/4 oz **mushrooms**, sliced

300 g/11 oz/medium can of **condensed mushroom soup**

5 ml/1 tsp **dried marjoram**

Salt and freshly ground black pepper

1   Preheat the slow cooker on High.

2   Heat the oil and butter or margarine in a large frying pan and fry the onions, garlic and green pepper gently for 2–3 minutes.

3   Stir in the lamb and cook until browned on all sides.

4   Stir in the mushrooms, soup and marjoram and season to taste with salt and pepper. Bring to the boil, then transfer to the slow cooker.

5   Cook on Low for 6–9 hours.

6   Serve with boiled potatoes and purple sprouting broccoli.

freezing tip
• Cook without the garlic. Add the crushed garlic when reheating.

lamb shanks in burgundy

4

10 MINS

8 hrs LOW

Mashed potatoes and a green vegetable

4 **lamb shanks**

Salt and freshly ground black pepper

5 ml/1 tsp **dried parsley flakes**

10 ml/2 tsp **garlic granules**

2.5 ml/½ tsp **dried oregano**

Grated zest of ½ **lemon**

1 **small onion**, chopped

1 **large carrot**, chopped

5 ml/1 tsp **olive oil**

250 ml/8 fl oz/1 cup **Burgundy wine**

5 ml/1 tsp **beef bouillon granules** or ½ **beef stock cube**, crumbled

1   Sprinkle the lamb with salt and pepper and place in the slow cooker. Sprinkle with the parsley, garlic, oregano and lemon zest.

2   In a small saucepan, sauté the onion and carrot in oil for 3-4 minutes or until tender. Stir in the wine and bouillon or stock cube. Bring to the boil, stirring occasionally. Pour over the lamb.

3   Cook on low for 8 hours or until the meat is tender.

4   Remove the lamb and keep warm. Strain the cooking juices and skim off the fat. Bring the juices to a boil in a small saucepan and cook until the liquid is reduced by half.

5   Serve the lamb with the sauce and mashed potatoes and a green vegetable.

honeyed leg of lamb

8 **10 MINS** **5-7 hrs HIGH** Roast vegetables

128
meat

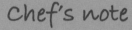

Chef's note

Lamb and honey is a combination fit for the gods! You might associate a cider-based sauce with pork but it works really well in this lamb dish too.

40 g/1½ oz/3 tbsp **butter or margarine**

2 kg/4½ lb **leg of lamb**

Salt and freshly ground black pepper

15 ml/1 tbsp **cornflour (cornstarch)**

A large pinch of **ground ginger**

300 ml/½ pt/1¼ cups **dry cider**

60 ml/4 tbsp **clear honey**

15 ml/1 tbsp **rosemary leaves**

1   Preheat the slow cooker on High.

2   Heat the butter or margarine in a large frying pan and brown the lamb on all sides. Season with salt and pepper and transfer to the slow cooker.

3   Stir the cornflour and ginger into the butter in the pan and mix well, then stir in the cider and honey and bring to the boil, stirring continuously. Pour over the lamb, making sure it is well covered. Sprinkle with the rosemary.

4   Cook on High for 5–7 hours, basting once or twice during cooking if possible.

5   Place the joint on a carving dish and serve the sauce separately.

6   Serve with roast vegetables.

freezing tip
• Leftover slices of lamb can be frozen in a foil tray with some of the sauce poured over.

navarin of lamb

6-8

10 MINS

7-10 hrs LOW

Boiled potatoes and carrots

1 kg/2½ lb **best end of neck of lamb chops**

Salt and freshly ground black pepper

15 g/½ oz/1 tsbp **butter or margarine**

3 **large carrots**, sliced

2 **onions**, chopped

450 g/1 lb **potatoes**, cut into 1 cm/½ in cubes

30 ml/2 tbsp **plain (all-purpose) flour**

600 ml/1 pt/2½ cups **beef stock**

10 ml/2 tsp **caster (superfine) sugar**

45 ml/3 tbsp **tomato purée (paste)**

1 **bouquet garni** sachet

1   Preheat the slow cooker on High.

2   Season the lamb chops with salt and pepper. Melt the butter or margarine in a frying pan , then brown the chops quickly on both sides. Transfer to the slow cooker.

3   Add the vegetables to the pan and cook gently for 4 minutes.

4   Mix the flour with a little of the stock, then mix in the remainder. Add to the vegetables in the pan with the remaining ingredients and bring to the boil, stirring continuously. Transfer to the slow cooker and stir well.

5   Cook on Low for 7–10 hours.

6   Discard the bouquet garni and adjust the seasoning before serving with boiled potatoes and carrots.

traditional liver & bacon

4   **15** MINS   **6-8** hrs LOW   Mashed potatoes and cabbage

45 ml/3 tbsp **plain (all-purpose) flour**

Salt and freshly ground black pepper

450 g/1 lb **lambs' liver**, cut into 1 cm/½ in slices

30 ml/2 tbsp **oil**

8 **back bacon rashers (slices)**

1 **onion**, chopped

150 ml/¼ pt/⅔ cup **beef stock**

15 g/½ oz/1 tbsp **butter** or **margarine**

1   Preheat the slow cooker on High.

2   Season 30 ml/2 tbsp of the flour with salt and pepper, then toss the liver in the flour, shaking off any excess.

3   Heat the oil in a frying pan and fry the bacon rashers and onion for 2–3 minutes. Drain off the fat, then transfer the bacon and onion to the slow cooker.

4   Lightly fry the liver in the pan until just sealed on all sides, then transfer to the slow cooker.

5   Stir the stock into the pan and bring to the boil. Season with salt and pepper, then pour into the slow cooker.

6   Cook on Low for 6–8 hours.

7   Blend together the butter or margarine and remaining flour to make a *beurre manié*. Half an hour before the dish is ready, drop pieces of the *beurre manié* into the slow cooker and stir well to thicken the sauce.

8   Serve with mashed potatoes and cabbage.

pork with apple in cider

4 · **15 MINS** · **6-10hrs LOW** · **Sauté potatoes**

15 ml/1 tbsp **oil**

25 g/1 oz/2 tbsp **butter or margarine**

1 **onion**, sliced

2 **celery sticks**, sliced

1 **large cooking (tart) apple**, peeled, cored and chopped

750 g/1¾ lb **lean pork**, cubed

30 ml/2 tbsp **plain (all-purpose) flour**

300 ml/½ pt/1¼ cups **dry cider**

Salt and freshly ground black pepper

1 **bouquet garni** sachet

1   Preheat the slow cooker on High.

2   Heat the oil and butter or margarine in a large pan and fry the onion, celery and apple gently for 2–3 minutes. Transfer to the slow cooker.

3   Add the pork to the pan and brown lightly.

4   Mix the flour with a little of the cider, then stir in the rest until well blended. Stir into the pan and bring to the boil, stirring continuously. Transfer to the slow cooker and stir well. Season with salt and pepper and add the bouquet garni.

5   Cook on Low for 6–10 hours.

6   Discard the bouquet garni before serving with sauté potatoes.

sweet & sour pork chops

4   **10** MINS   **5-8** hrs LOW   Rice or egg noodles

Chef's note

This is a lovely way to cook pork chops and is inspired by Chinese cuisine. Serve the chops and the sauce with plain boiled rice or with egg noodles.

15 ml/1 tbsp **plain (all-purpose) flour**

Salt and freshly ground black pepper

4 **pork chops**, trimmed

50 g/2 oz/¼ cup **butter or margarine**

2 **onions**, finely chopped

60 ml/4 tbsp **soy sauce**

60 ml/4 tbsp **tomato purée (paste)**

60 ml/4 tbsp **soft brown sugar**

150 ml/¼ pt/⅔ cup **dry sherry**

1   Preheat the slow cooker on High.

2   Season the flour with salt and pepper, then dust the chops with the flour, shaking off any excess.

3   Heat the butter or margarine in a frying pan and brown the chops quickly on all sides. Transfer to the slow cooker.

4   Add the onions to the pan and fry gently until transparent.

5   Stir in the remaining ingredients and bring to the boil, then pour over the chops in the slow cooker.

6   Cook on Low for 5–8 hours.

7   Serve with rice or egg noodles.

pork & pineapple curry

6 | **10** MINS | **5-8** hrs LOW | Rice

Chef's note

The flavour combinations in this curry are terrific – the heat of the curry powder and chillies is softened and sweetened by the pineapple and mango chutney. Simple plain boiled rice is all it needs for the perfect accompaniment.

45 ml/3 tbsp **plain (all-purpose) flour**

5 ml/1 tsp **salt**

1 kg/2¼ lb **lean pork**, cubed

30 ml/2 tbsp **oil**

1 **large onion**, finely chopped

15 ml/1 tbsp **curry powder**

15 ml/1 tbsp **ground paprika**

300 ml/½ pt/1¼ cups **chicken stock**

2 dried **red chillies**

15 ml/1 tbsp **mango chutney**

5 ml/1 tsp **Worcestershire sauce**

400 g/14 oz/large can of **pineapple cubes in syrup**

2 **bay leaves**

1   Preheat the slow cooker on High.

2   Heat the oil and butter or margarine in a large pan and fry the onion, celery and apple gently for 2–3 minutes. Transfer to the slow cooker.

3   Add the pork to the pan and brown lightly.

4   Mix the flour with a little of the cider, then stir in the rest until well blended. Stir into the pan and bring to the boil, stirring continuously. Transfer to the slow cooker and stir well. Season with salt and pepper and add the bouquet garni.

5   Cook on Low for 5–8 hours.

6   Discard the bouquet garni before serving with rice.

spiced spare ribs

6   **15** MINS   **6-8** hrs LOW   Rice

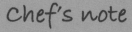

Chef's note

Spare ribs are the most inexpensive cut of pork ribs but are also one of the most delicious, especially when, as here, they are slow-cooked so the meat that covers and lies between the bones is tender and bathed in a delicious sauce.

15 ml/1 tbsp **plain (all-purpose) flour**

Salt and freshly ground black pepper

1 kg/2¼ lb **pork spare ribs**

30 ml/2 tbsp **oil**

1 **onion**, finely chopped

1 **green (bell) pepper**, seeded and finely chopped

1 **garlic clove**, crushed

300 ml/½ pt/1¼ cups **lager**

30 ml/2 tbsp **tomato purée (paste)**

60 ml/4 tbsp **Worcestershire sauce**

A few drops of **Tabasco sauce**

1   Preheat the slow cooker on High.

2   Season the flour with salt and pepper, then dust the spare ribs with the flour, shaking off any excess.

3   Heat the oil in a frying pan and fry the spare ribs quickly until browned on all sides. Transfer to the slow cooker.

4   Add the onion, pepper and garlic to the pan and fry gently for 3–4 minutes.

5   Stir in the remaining ingredients, bring to the boil, then pour over the ribs in the slow cooker.

6   Cook on Low for 6–8 hours.

7   Serve with rice.

chinese-style pork

4

20 MINS

6-8 hrs LOW

Rice

10 ml/2 tsp **ground paprika**

1 kg/2¼ lb **boneless pork loin**, cut into 2.5 cm/1 in strips

15 ml/1 tbsp **sesame oil**

550 g/1¼ lb/very large can of **unsweetened pineapple chunks**

1 **large onion**, chopped

2 **green (bell) peppers**, chopped

60 ml/4 tbsp **cider vinegar**

40 g/1½ oz **brown sugar**

45 ml/3 tsbp **soy sauce**

15 ml/1 tbsp **Worcestershire sauce**

2.5 ml/½ tsp **salt**

15 g/½ oz **cornflour (cornstarch)**

60 ml/4 tbsp **water**

1   Place the paprika in a large plastic bag. Add the pork, a few pieces at a time, and shake to coat. Heat the oil in a non-stick frying pan and brown the pork, then transfer to the slow cooker.

2   Drain the pineapple, reserving the juice. Add the pineapple juice, onion, green pepper, vinegar, brown sugar, soy sauce, Worcestershire sauce and salt to the slow cooker and mix well. Cook on Low for 6–8 hours or until the meat is tender.

3   Combine the cornflour and water until smooth, stir into the pork mixture and add the pineapple. Cook for 30 minutes or until the sauce has thickened.

4   Serve spooned over rice.

easy cassoulet

4 | **10** MINS | **8-10**hrs LOW | Crusty baguette

Chef's note

Cassoulet is a rich stew containing haricot beans and various meats. In southern France, where it originates, it might include goose, duck and mutton as well as the pork and sausage used here. Remember to allow for cooking the beans overnight in the slow cooker.

450 g/1 lb **dried haricot (navy) beans**

1 **bay leaf**, crushed

2 **garlic cloves**, crushed

2.5 ml/½ tsp **dried thyme**

2.5 ml/½ tsp **dried sage**

Salt and freshly ground black pepper

450 g/1 lb **belly pork**, rinded and cubed

350 g/12 oz **Toulouse or other spicy sausages**

250 ml/8 fl oz/1 cup **chicken stock**

100 g/4 oz/2 cups **fresh breadcrumbs**

50 g/2 oz/½ cup **grated strong cheese**

To thicken (optional)

15 ml/1 tbsp **plain (all-purpose) flour**

15 ml/1 tbsp **butter or margarine**

1   Preheat the slow cooker on High.

2   Place the beans in the slow cooker and cover with cold water. Cook on Low overnight until soft.

3   Drain the beans, then return to the slow cooker with the bay leaf, garlic, thyme, sage and seasoning.

4   Heat a frying pan and fry the pork until sealed on all sides. Stir into the beans.

5   In the same pan, fry the sausages until lightly browned, then place on top of the beans.

6   Pour the stock into the pan, bring to the boil, then pour into the slow cooker. Cook on Low for 8–10 hours.

7   If you wish to thicken the cassoulet, half an hour before serving mix together the flour and butter to make a *beurre manié* (see page 132) and stir it into the cassoulet.

8   Mix together the breadcrumbs and cheese and sprinkle over the cassoulet. Brown under a hot grill (broiler) for a few minutes.

9   Serve with crusty bread.

piquant bacon in wine

There are more ways to enjoy bacon than just fried for breakfast or in a roll! Here it is cooked with onion and carrots in a juice spiced with pepper and cloves to excite the taste buds.

6 | **20** MINS | **7-10**hrs LOW | Potatoes and peas

1 kg/2¼ lb **unsmoked bacon**, rinded and cubed

50 g/2 oz/¼ cup **butter or margarine**

1 **large onion**, chopped

2 **carrots**, sliced

30 ml/2 tbsp **plain (all-purpose) flour**

300 ml/½ pt/1¼ cups **dry white wine or chicken stock**

45 ml/3 tbsp **wine vinegar**

2.5 ml/½ tsp **freshly ground black pepper**

A pinch of **ground cloves**

1   Preheat the slow cooker on High.

2   Place the bacon cubes in a saucepan and cover with cold water. Bring slowly to the boil. Discard the water and pat the bacon dry on kitchen paper (paper towels).

3   Heat the butter or margarine in a frying pan and brown the bacon lightly on all sides. Transfer to the slow cooker.

4   Add the onion and carrots to the frying pan and fry for a few minutes. Stir in the flour, then gradually add the chicken stock or wine and the vinegar. Bring to the boil, then add the pepper and cloves. Transfer to the slow cooker and stir well.

5   Cook on Low for 7–10 hours.

6   Serve with potatoes and peas.

braised gammon

6   **20** MINS   **3-5** hrs HIGH   **Potatoes**

Chef's note

Gammon is a lovely joint to enjoy on Boxing Day, and slow cooking it means you can have a rest from all the frantic kitchen activity of the day before. Boiling the gammon before the slow cooking will ensure it is not over-salty.

1 kg/2¼ lb **bacon or gammon joint**

15 ml/1 tbsp **brown sugar**

225 g/8 oz **tomatoes,** skinned and coarsely chopped

2 **onions**, thinly sliced

Freshly ground black pepper

60 ml/4 tbsp **water**

100 g/4 oz **button mushrooms**, sliced

30 ml/2 tbsp **lemon juice**

15 ml/1 tbsp **chopped fresh parsley**

1   Preheat the slow cooker on High.

2   Place the joint in a saucepan and cover with cold water. Bring slowly to the boil, then discard the water and remove the bacon from the pan.

3   Cut off the rind and snip the remaining fat at intervals. Sprinkle the joint with the brown sugar and place under a preheated grill (broiler) to melt and brown.

4   Layer the tomato and onion slices in the slow cooker, season with pepper and add half the water. Place the bacon joint on top.

5   Cook on High for 3–5 hours.

6   In a separate saucepan, cook the mushrooms in the remaining water and the lemon juice for about 4 minutes, then drain.

7   Garnish the bacon with the mushrooms and parsley and serve with potatoes.

freezing tip
• Freeze without the mushroom and parsley garnish.

poultry & game

Slow cooking poultry and game guarantees that remains moist and tender, with no danger of the dryin out that can happen during conventional cooking. Yo can cook whole birds, joints or pieces, and the slo cooker will tenderise even the toughest birds with n loss of flavour.

The size of your slow cooker will obviously determin the size of bird you will be able to cook. A 2.5 litre $4\frac{1}{2}$ pt pot will accommodate a 1.75 kg/4 lb bird.

Thaw frozen poultry completely before slow cookin Frozen cooked poultry dishes are best defrosted a room temperature, then reheated gently bu thoroughly in the oven just before serving.

Poultry and game tips

- Always cook whole birds on High.

- Avoid overcooking as the bones will begin to fall apart if the dish is left to cook for too long.

- Light browning before cooking will improve both the flavour and appearance of poultry dishes.

- Whole birds are best trussed so that they can easily be removed from the pot when cooked.

- Make sure that vegetables are cut into small pieces so that they cook in time.

- Season lightly before cooking, then adjust the seasoning to taste before serving.

- Use about half the liquid specified in conventional recipes if you adapt them for the slow cooker.

- You can use stock, water, wine, cider or fruit juice for slow cooking poultry.

- Thicken dishes before cooking or for the last 1–1½ hours (see page 12).

- Add egg yolks, cream or milk for only the last 30 minutes of the cooking time.

chilli & ginger chicken

4   **10 MINS**   **5-8 hrs LOW**   **Pasta or rice**

Chef's note

Chilli and ginger really do add an exciting tang to chicken, which is sweetened and beautifully balanced by the addition of pineapple. This dish would be lovely served with Thai fragrant rice.

50 g/2 oz/¼ cup **butter or margarine**

4 **chicken portions**

1 **onion**, chopped

2 **celery sticks**, chopped

30 ml/2 tbsp **plain (all-purpose) flour**

150 ml/¼ pt/⅔ cup **chicken stock**

450 g/14 oz/large can of **pineapple pieces in juice**

10 ml/2 tbsp **chilli powder**

2.5 ml/½ tsp **ground ginger**

A few drops of **Tabasco sauce**

Salt and freshly ground black pepper

1   Preheat the slow cooker on High.

2   Heat the butter or margarine in a frying pan and brown the chicken portions on all sides. Transfer to the slow cooker.

3   Add the onion and celery to the pan and fry until transparent.

4   Stir in the flour, then gradually stir in the stock, the pineapple and juice and all the remaining ingredients and bring to the boil, stirring continuously. Pour over the chicken.

5   Cook on Low for 5–8 hours.

6   Serve with pasta or rice.

curried chicken legs

4   **15** MINS   **6-8** hrs LOW   Naan bread and spicy indian chutneys

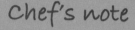

Chef's note

Chicken leg joints are often overlooked in favour of more expensive breasts, but they are the perfect choice – and more than a match – for the robust fruited curry sauce in this recipe.

30 ml/2 tbsp **oil**

4 **chicken legs**, skinned

Salt and freshly ground black pepper

1 **onion**, chopped

1 **garlic clove**, crushed

50 g/2 oz/⅓ cup **sultanas (golden raisins)**

30 ml/2 tbsp **curry powder**

30 ml/2 tbsp **plain (all-purpose) flour**

150 ml/¼ pt/⅔ cup **chicken stock**

1   Preheat the slow cooker on High.

2   Heat the oil in a frying pan and lightly brown the chicken legs on all sides. Remove from the pan with a slotted spoon, season with salt and pepper and place in the slow cooker.

3   Add the onion and garlic to the pan and fry until transparent, then stir in the sultanas. Transfer to the slow cooker.

4   Stir the curry powder and flour into the pan and fry gently for 2 minutes, stirring continuously. Gradually add the stock, stirring all the time, and bring to the boil, then pour into the slow cooker.

5   Cook on Low for 6–8 hours.

6   Serve with naan bread and spicy Indian chutneys.

coq au vin

4 · **15 MINS** · **6-8 hrs LOW** · **Duchesse potatoes**

Chef's note

This is a classic dish that has its roots in French country cookery. It was an early favourite in the UK and elsewhere when interest in European cuisines first began to flourish in the mid-twentieth century – and its popularity has never diminished since then.

50 g/2 oz/¼ cup **butter or margarine**

4 **chicken portions**, skinned

2 **onions**, chopped

1 **garlic clove**, crushed

4 **streaky bacon rashers (slices)**, rinded and chopped

100 g/4 oz **button mushrooms**, halved

50 g/2 oz/½ cup **plain (all-purpose) flour**

150 ml/¼ pt/⅔ cup **chicken stock**

300 ml/½ pt/1¼ cups **red wine**

2 **bay leaves**

1 **bouquet garni** sachet

Salt and freshly ground black pepper

1   Preheat the slow cooker on High.

2   Heat the butter or margarine in a frying pan and brown the chicken pieces on all sides. Transfer to the slow cooker.

3   Add the onion, garlic and bacon to the pan and fry gently until transparent.

4   Stir in the mushrooms, then the flour and cook for 1 minute, then stir in the stock and wine and bring to the boil. Add the bay leaves and bouquet garni and season with salt and pepper. Transfer to the slow cooker.

5   Cook on Low for 6–8 hours.

6   Discard the bay leaves and bouquet garni before serving.

7   Serve with duchesse potatoes.

chicken casserole

4

15 MINS

6-8 hrs LOW

Jacket potatoes and carrots

Chef's note

One of the all-time greats, with almost as many variations as there are kitchens to create it in. This version includes carrots, celery, sweetcorn and peppers but you can ring the changes and use whatever vegetables you like or have to hand.

---

50 g/2 oz/¼ cup **butter or margarine**

4 **chicken portions**

2 **onions**, chopped

1 **garlic clove**, crushed

2 **streaky bacon rashers (slices)**, rinded and chopped

2 **carrots**, chopped

2 **celery sticks**, chopped

30 ml/2 tbsp **plain (all-purpose) flour**

450 ml/¾ pt/2 cups **chicken stock**

30 ml/2 tbsp **tomato purée (paste)**

1 **bouquet garni** sachet

Salt and freshly ground black pepper

225 g/8 oz **mixed frozen sweetcorn (corn) and chopped (bell) peppers**

1   Preheat the slow cooker on High.

2   Heat the butter or margarine in a frying pan and brown the chicken on all sides. Transfer to the slow cooker.

3   Add the onions, garlic, bacon, carrots and celery to the pan and fry for 4 minutes.

4   Stir in the flour, then gradually stir in the stock, tomato purée, bouquet garni and seasoning and bring to the boil, stirring continuously. Pour over the chicken.

5   Cook on Low for 6–8 hours.

6   About 30 minutes before serving, stir in the sweetcorn and peppers.

7   Discard the bouquet garni and adjust the seasoning before serving with jacket potatoes and carrots.

freezer tip

• Omit the garlic when slow cooking, then add the garlic or season with garlic salt when reheating.

parsley roast chicken

6

10 MINS

4-5 hrs HIGH

Roast potatoes, stuffing and seasonal vegetables

1 **whole chicken,** about 1.75 kg/4 lb

2 **garlic cloves**, thinly sliced

Salt and freshly ground black pepper

60 ml/4 tbsp **oil**

100 g/4 oz/$\frac{1}{2}$ cup **butter or margarine**

45 ml/3 tbsp **chopped fresh parsley**

1   Preheat the slow cooker on High.

2   Using a sharp knife, cut small slits in the breasts and thighs of the chicken and insert the slivers of garlic. Season the bird with salt and pepper.

3   Heat the oil and butter or margarine in a large frying pan and brown the chicken on all sides. Transfer the chicken to the slow cooker.

4   Stir the parsley into the remaining butter or margarine in the pan, then pour over the chicken.

5   Cook on High for 4–5 hours.

6   Cover with foil and leave to rest for a few minutes before carving.

7   Serve with roast potatoes, stuffing and seasonal vegetables.

chicken & pepper risotto

Chef's note

Risottos are a wonderful dish, with endless variations on the onion, rice and stock foundation. Chicken and peppers together make one of the very best risottos and the slow cooker does away with standing over the hob stirring while it cooks.

4 | **15** MINS | **3-4** hrs LOW | Mixed green salad

30 ml/2 tbsp **oil**

2 **onions**, finely chopped

900 ml/1½ pts/3¾ cups **chicken stock**

1 **small green (bell) pepper**, seeded and chopped

1 **small red pepper**, seeded and chopped

100 g/4 oz **button mushrooms**

3 **tomatoes**, skinned and chopped

175 g/6 oz/¾ cup **easy-cook long grain rice**

225 g/8 oz **cooked chicken**, chopped

50 g/2 oz **cooked ham**, choppe

50 g/2 oz/½ cup **freshly grated Parmesan cheese**

1   Preheat the slow cooker on High.

2   Heat the oil in a large frying pan and fry the onions until transparent.

3   Add the stock and bring to the boil. Stir in the remaining ingredients except the Parmesan and return to the boil, then transfer to the slow cooker.

4   Cook on Low for 3–4 hours.

5   Stir well and sprinkle with the Parmesan.

6   Serve with a mixed green salad.

chicken in orange sauce

Chef's note

You might associate an orange sauce more with duck, but until you try it you won't appreciate how well it complements chicken too. And this recipe is so simple, there's really no reason not to!

4 | **10 MINS** | **5 hrs LOW** | Rice

1 **whole chicken**, about 1.25 kg/ 2½ lb, jointed and skin removed

750 ml/1¼ pts/3 cups **orange juice**

3 **celery sticks**, chopped

1 **large green (bell) pepper**, chopped

100 g/4 oz **mushrooms**, chopped

5 ml/1 tsp **dried onion flakes**

15 ml/1 tbsp **chopped fresh parsley**

Salt and freshly ground black pepper

30 ml/1 tbsp **cornflour (cornstarch)**

45 ml/3 tbsp **water**

1   Combine all the ingredients except the cornflour and water in the slow cooker.

2   Cook on Low for 4 hours or until the meat juices run clear.

3   Combine the cornflour and water until smooth, then stir into the cooking juices.

4   Cook on high for 30–45 minutes or until thickened.

5   Serve spooned over rice.

lemon & cream chicken

4   **15 MINS**   **6-8 hrs LOW**   Pasta shapes

Chef's note

A truly luscious chicken dish, its creamy richness delicately balanced by the tartness of lemon. It lends itself to many accompaniments, but sautéed or simple boiled potatoes and a special salad would be good choices.

4 skinless, **boneless chicken breasts**

1 **garlic clove**, thinly sliced

Grated zest and juice of 1 **lemon**

Salt and freshly ground black pepper

25 g/1 oz/2 tbsp **butter or margarine**

30 ml/2 tbsp **oil**

30 ml/2 tbsp **single (light) cream**

15 ml/1 tbsp **chopped fresh parsley**

1   Preheat the slow cooker on High.

2   Make small cuts in the chicken breasts and insert slivers of garlic and a little lemon rind. Season the breasts with salt and pepper.

3   Heat the butter or margarine and oil in a frying pan and brown the chicken breasts quickly on all sides. Transfer from the pan to the slow cooker.

4   Stir the lemon juice into the pan and bring to the boil, then pour over the chicken.

5   Cook on Low for 6–8 hours.

6   Half an hour before serving, stir in the cream and parsley.

7   Serve with pasta shapes.

garlic & lemon chicken

6 **5** MINS **8-10**hrs LOW Rice

Chef's note

This recipe just couldn't be simpler to prepare – you just mix everything together and pour it over the chicken – and yet the results are so delicious. This is a chicken dish that would freeze very well, in the unlikely event that you had any left over!

750 ml/1¼ pts/3 cups **white wine**

350 ml/12 fl oz/1⅓ cups **lemon juice**

1 **head of garlic**, crushed

4 drops of **hot pepper sauce**

A pinch of **poultry seasoning**

7.5 ml/1½ tsp **salt**

6 **skinless, boneless chicken breasts**

1   Combine all the ingredients except the chicken and mix
    thoroughly.

2   Place the chicken in slow cooker and pour the lemon and
    garlic mixture over.

3   Cook on Low for 8–10 hours.

4   Serve with rice.

chinese chicken

4

10 MINS

8-10 hrs LOW

Egg fried rice

4 **chicken pieces**, skinned

Salt and freshly ground black pepper

30 ml/2 tbsp **oil**

1 **onion**, chopped

1 **red (bell) pepper**, seeded and chopped

300 ml/½ pt/1¼ cups **chicken stock**

15 ml/1 tbsp **soft brown sugar**

15 ml/1 tbsp **soy sauce**

2.5 ml/½ tsp **ground ginger**

300 g/11 oz/medium can of **pineapple cubes**, drained

10 ml/2 tsp **cornflour (cornstarch)**

15 ml/1 tbsp **water**

1   Preheat the slow cooker on High.

2   Season the chicken with salt and pepper. Heat the oil in a frying pan and brown the chicken quickly on all sides, then transfer to the slow cooker.

3   Stir all the remaining ingredients except the cornflour and water into the pan, stir together well and heat through, then transfer to the slow cooker.

4   Cook on Low for 8–10 hours.

5   Half an hour before serving, blend the cornflour with the water, then stir it into the slow cooker to thicken the sauce.

6   Serve with egg fried rice.

chicken creole

4 **10 MINS** **5-6 hrs HIGH** **Sweet potatoes**

Chef's note

This is one of the classics of Lousiana cuisine, which has – among others – French, Spanish and Caribbean influences. It's an easy and tasty dish, perfect over egg noodles, but any leftovers can be bumped up with extra veggies and water as necessary to make an appetising soup.

4 **skinless, boneless chicken breasts,** halved

Salt and freshly ground black pepper

Creole-style seasoning

400 g/14 oz/large can of **chopped tomatoes**

1 **celery stalk**, diced

1 **green (bell) pepper**, diced

3 **garlic cloves**, crushed

1 **onion**, finely chopped

100 g/4 oz **mushrooms**, chopped

1 **fresh jalapeno pepper**, seeded and chopped

1   Place the chicken breasts in the slow cooker. Season with salt, pepper and Creole-style seasoning to taste.

2   Stir in the tomatoes with their liquid, the celery, diced pepper, garlic, onion, mushrooms and jalapeno pepper.

3   Cook on High for 5–6 hours, or on Low for 10–12 hours.

4   Serve with sweet potatoes.

paella

Chef's note

Paella is a Spanish dish, the essential ingredients of which are rice, vegetables and saffron. It was a difficult choice whether this paella mixta belonged in the chicken or the seafood section as it uses a perfect balance of both.

6

15 MINS

3-4 hrs LOW

Complete meal in itself

30 ml/2 tbsp **olive oil**

1 **onion**, finely chopped

1 **garlic clove**, crushed

900 ml/1½ pts/3¾ cups **chicken stock**

A pinch of **ground saffron**

225 g/8 oz/1 cup **easy-cook long-grain rice**

4 **tomatoes**, skinned and chopped

1 **red (bell) pepper**, seeded and finely chopped

225 g/8 oz **cooked chicken**, chopped

Salt and freshly ground black

pepper

6 **cooked mussels**

6 **cooked prawns (shrimp)**

100 g/4 oz **frozen peas**, thawed

1   Preheat the slow cooker on High.

2   Heat the oil in a large frying pan and fry the onion and garlic until transparent.

3   Add the stock and saffron, bring to the boil, then stir in all the remaining ingredients except the mussels, prawns and peas, seasoning with salt and pepper. Return to the boil, then transfer to the slow cooker.

4   Cook on Low for 3–4 hours.

5   Half an hour before serving, stir in the mussels, prawns and peas.

pheasant in cider

4

20 MINS

3-4 hrs HIGH

Mashed potatoes and a green vegetable

Chef's note

If you're an inexperienced or reluctant game bird cook, this slow-cooker recipe is the ideal way to overcome any reservations. It's a little more complicated than some of the recipes in this chapter and needs some end-game effort, but the results will be impressive.

30 ml/2 tbsp **plain (all-purpose) flour**

Salt and freshly ground black pepper

1 **large pheasant**

50 g/2 oz/¼ cup **butter or margarine**

1 **onion**, finely chopped

1 **garlic clove**, crushed

300 ml/½ pt/1¼ cups **dry cider**

1 **bouquet garni** sachet

4 **streaky bacon rashers (slices)**, rinded

2 **eating (dessert) apples**

15 ml/1 tbsp **lemon juice**

60 ml/4 tbsp **soured (dairy sour) cream**

5 ml/1 tsp **ground paprika**

1   Preheat the slow cooker on High. Season the flour with salt and pepper. Dust the pheasant in half the flour, shaking off any excess.

2   Heat half the butter or margarine in a large frying pan and brown the pheasant on all sides. Transfer to the slow cooker.

3   In the same pan, fry the onion and garlic gently until transparent. Stir in the remaining flour and cook for 1 minute, then gradually stir in the cider and bring to the boil. Add the bouquet garni and season with salt and pepper. Pour over the pheasant. Cook on High for 3–4 hours.

4   Lift the pheasant from the slow cooker, cover with foil and leave to rest.

5   Heat the remaining butter or margarine in a pan. Roll up the bacon rashers and fry in the butter until crisp.

6   Peel, core and quarter the apples and immediately toss in the lemon juice. Add to the pan and fry until golden.

7   Strain the pheasant cooking juices and reheat in a pan, then stir in the soured cream and paprika. Do not boil.

8   Serve the pheasant garnished with the sauce, bacon and apples with mashed potatoes and a green vegetable.

turkey in a cream sauce

6

20 **MINS**

6-8 hrs **LOW**

Tagliatelle

25 g/1 oz/2 tbsp **butter or margarine**

450 g/1 lb **turkey meat**, cubed

1 **onion**, thinly sliced

3 **celery sticks**, chopped

2 **carrots**, chopped

30 ml/2 tbsp **plain (all-purpose) flour**

300 ml/½ pt/1¼ cups **chicken stock**

1 **bouquet garni** sachet

Salt and freshly ground black pepper

150 ml/¼ pt/⅔ cup **single (light) cream**

1   Preheat the slow cooker on High.

2   Heat the butter or margarine in a frying pan and fry the turkey gently until sealed on all sides, then transfer to the slow cooker.

3   Add the onion, celery and carrots to the pan and fry for 3–4 minutes.

4   Stir in the flour and cook for 1 minute, then gradually stir in the stock and bring to the boil. Add the bouquet garni and season with salt and pepper. Pour over the turkey.

5   Cook on Low for 6–8 hours.

6   Half an hour before serving, stir in the cream.

7   Serve with tagliatelle.

freezing tip
• Freeze without the cream. Stir in the cream during reheating.

traditional venison stew

Chef's note

Deer meat is called venison, whether it is hunted or farmed. It is much lower in calories, cholesterol and fat than most cuts of beef (which its taste resembles), so this easy-to-make venison stew is an all-round healthy choice.

3 **celery stalks**, diced

1 **onion**, chopped

2 **garlic cloves**, crushed

10 ml/2 tsp **chopped fresh parsley**

30 ml/2 tsbp **vegetable oil**

900 g/2 lb **venison stewing meat**

Salt and freshly ground black pepper

5 ml/1 tsp **dried oregano**

15 ml/1 tbsp **chopped fresh basil**

250 ml/8 fl oz/1 cup **tomato sauce**

120 ml/4 fl oz/½ cup **dry red wine**

120 ml/4 fl oz/½ cup **water**

1   Place the celery, onion, garlic, and parsley in the slow cooker. Heat the oil in a large frying pan over medium-high heat. Brown the venison well in two batches and add to the slow cooker.

2   Add salt and pepper to taste, the oregano and basil. Pour in the tomato sauce, red wine and water.

3   Cook on Low for 7–10 hours.

4   Serve with jacket potatoes and seasonal vegetables.

shredded venison tacos

4

10 MINS

8 hrs LOW

Taco shells, lettuce, tomato, onion, grated cheese

Chef's note

You can serve healthy venison in tacos as a tasty alternative to the more usual beef. Once shredded, serve the meat with taco shells, lettuce, tomato, onion, cheese and taco sauce.

30 g/1¼ oz pack of **taco seasoning**

30 ml/1 tbsp **plain (all-purpose) flour**

750 g/1¾ lb **venison roasting joint**

Cayenne pepper

15 ml/1 tbsp **vegetable oil**

200 ml/7 fl oz/scant 1 cup **water**

Salt and freshly ground black pepper

1 Mix half the taco seasoning with the flour and cayenne pepper to taste and coat the meat with this mixture.

2 Heat the oil in a large frying pan over medium-high heat. Place the roast in the oil and brown well on all sides.

3 Place the meat in the slow cooker with the water and cook on Low for 8 hours or on High for 5 hours.

4 When the meat is done, shred it with a fork and season to taste.

5 Serve in taco shells with lettuce, tomato and onion and top with grated cheese.

vegetables

Vegetable flavours are delicate, so it is good to kn
that they are sealed in during slow cooking and gen
but surely developed within the pot. You may find th
the texture differs slightly from vegetables cook
conventionally but you will most certainly note a
appreciate the improved flavours. Fresh, frozen a
dried vegetables are all suitable for slow cooking.

Some of the recipes in this chapter are suitable f
main dishes, others will make delicious side dish
or starters.

Frozen vegetables should be thawed before adding
the slow cooker. In order to retain their full colour a
texture, stir them into a recipe during the final
minutes of cooking. This will also avoid suddenly a
drastically lowering the temperature within the sl
cooker.

Slow cooked vegetables can be frozen, particularly
cooked in a sauce, though you may not feel it is wo
it for some recipes. Remember that vegetables tend
lose some of their flavour and texture on freezi
and reheating.

vegetable tips

- Vegetables generally require a longer cooking time in the slow cooker than when cooked conventionally. Cut them into small pieces about 5 mm/¼ in thick, particularly in recipes that combine vegetables and meat. Try to ensure that the pieces are of even size.

- Root vegetables such as potatoes, carrots, turnips and onions usually require a cooking time of at least 6 hours on Low.

- Vegetables, especially potatoes, should be just covered in liquid while slow cooking.

- Pre-cooked vegetables can be added to a recipe 30 minutes before serving.

- Do not over-season as vegetables will retain all their concentrated flavours. Check and adjust the seasoning before serving.

- When adapting conventional recipes, reduce the amount of liquid used. You may also need to reduce the quantity of strongly flavoured vegetables, such as leeks or onions.

- Thickening agents such as flour and cornflour (cornstarch) can be added at the start of cooking (see page 12). Add cream, milk or egg yolks during the final 30 minutes.

- If a recipe includes dried peas or beans, they should be soaked overnight in cold water before cooking. Drain and rinse the beans, then cover in fresh water and boil rapidly for 15 minutes to destroy any natural toxins in the pulses. Always season after cooking as salt causes the beans to harden during cooking. Soaking is not necessary for lentils.

ratatouille

This classic stewed vegetable dish originated in the Provençal region of France. It makes a hearty side dish but can also be a nutritious main course, perhaps topped with Parmesan shavings, or it can be used as a base for a vegetarian lasagne.

4   **10** MINS   **5-8** hrs LOW

120 ml/4 fl oz/½ cup **olive oil**

1 **large onion**, finely chopped

1 **green (bell) pepper**, seeded and sliced

1 **red pepper**, seeded and sliced

1 **large aubergine (eggplant)**, diced

3 **courgettes (zucchini)**, thickly sliced

450 g/1 lb **tomatoes**, skinned, seeded and chopped or 400 g/14 oz/large can of **chopped tomatoes**

2 **garlic cloves**, crushed

Salt and freshly ground black pepper

A few **basil leaves**, torn

15 ml/1 tbsp **chopped fresh parsley**

1   Preheat the slow cooker on High.

2   Heat the oil in a large frying pan or saucepan and fry the onion and peppers until soft but not browned.

3   Add all the remaining ingredients except the herbs and season with salt and pepper. Heat through, turning the vegetables thoroughly in the oil. Transfer to the slow cooker.

4   Cook on Low for 5–8 hours.

5   Stir in the basil and parsley and serve hot or cold as a side dish or starter.

garden vegetables

4 **10** MINS **4-5** hrs LOW

Chef's note

A superb medly of wholesome vegetables to enjoy as a side dish or a simple lunch or supper. Tapioca is gluten-free and has almost no flavour of its own; it acts as a thickener and in this recipe it absorbs the delightful flavours of the vegetables.

2 **celery sticks**, cut into 2.5 cm/ 1 in pieces

2 **small carrots**, cut into 2.5 cm/ 1 in pieces

100 g/4 oz **tomatoes**, cut into chunks

1 **onion**, thinly sliced

100 g/4 oz fresh **green beans**, cut into 2.5 cm/1 in pieces

1 **green (bell) pepper**, cut into 2.5 cm/1 in pieces

25 g/1 oz/2 tbsp **butter or margarine**, melted

15 ml/1 tbsp **quick-cook tapioca**

5 ml/1 tsp **sugar**

Salt and freshly ground black pepper

1   Place the vegetables in the slow cooker.

2   Combine the butter, tapioca, sugar and salt and pepper to taste. Add to the vegetables and stir well.

3   Cover and cook on Low for 4–5 hours or until the vegetables are tender. Serve with a slotted spoon.

stuffed aubergines

4 · **75 MINS** · **5-6 hrs LOW**

Chef's note

Aubergines can be scooped out and stuffed with all manner of fillings; here we use breadcrumbs, onion and parsley to create a wonderful side dish or a main course to serve with rice or salad.

2 **aubergines (eggplants)**, halved lengthway

Salt and freshly ground black pepper

60 ml/4 tbsp **olive oil**

1 **onion**, chopped

1 **garlic clove**, crushed

1 **tomato**, skinned and chopped

15 ml/1 tbsp **chopped fresh parsley**

150 ml/¼ pt/⅔ cup **hot vegetable stock**

50 g/2 oz/1 cup **fresh breadcrumbs**

50 g/2 oz/½ cup **strong cheese**, grated

1   Sprinkle the aubergines with salt and leave to stand for 1 hour. Rinse and drain well.

2   Preheat the slow cooker on High.

3   Heat the oil in a large frying pan and fry the aubergines, cut-side down, until soft. Remove from the pan and scoop out the flesh, leaving the shells intact. Chop the flesh.

4   Fry the onion in the remaining oil until transparent, then remove from the heat and stir in the chopped aubergine, the garlic, tomatoes and parsley. Season with salt and pepper. Pile into the aubergine shells, place them in the slow cooker and pour the hot stock around.

5   Cook on Low for 5–6 hours.

6   Mix together the breadcrumbs and cheese and sprinkle over the aubergines. Brown under a hot grill (broiler) before serving.

barbecue-style beans

4

15 MINS

4-5 hrs LOW

225 g/8 oz **lean minced (ground) beef**

2 **bacon rashers (slices)**, chopped

1 **small onion**, finely chopped

450 g/1 lb/large can of **beans with pork**

200 g/7 oz/small can of **red kidney beans**

200 g/7 oz/small can of **butter (lima) beans**, partially drained

250 ml/8 fl oz/1 cup **tomato ketchup (catsup)**

15 ml/1 tbsp **liquid smoke flavouring**

15 ml/1 tbsp **salt**

15 ml/1 tbsp **hot sauce**

A good pinch of **garlic granule**

1   Preheat the slow cooker on High.

2   Place the beef in a large, deep frying pan. Stir over a medium-high heat until evenly browned and the grains have separated. Drain and set aside.

3   Place the bacon in the frying pan and cook over medium-high heat until evenly browned. Drain and set aside.

4   Combine the beef and bacon with all the remaining ingredients in the slow cooker.

5   Cook on Low for 4–5 hours.

slow creamed corn

4

10 MINS

4-6 hrs LOW

225 g/8 oz **frozen sweetcorn**

100 g/4 oz **cream cheese**

40 g/1½ oz/3 tbsp **butter**

45 ml/3 tbsp **milk**

5 ml/1 tsp **sugar**

Salt and freshly ground black pepper

1   Combine all the ingredients in the slow cooker, adding salt and pepper to taste.

2   Cook on Low for 4–6 hours or High for 2–4 hours.

freezing tip
- This dish freezes well.

courgettes hereford

4-6

10 MINS

4-6 hrs LOW

40 g/1½ oz/3 tbsp **butter or margarine**

450 g/1 lb **courgettes (zucchini)**, cut into 2.5 cm/1 in lengths

1 **garlic clove**, crushed

1 **small onion**, finely chopped

15 ml/1 tbsp **cornflour (cornstarch)**

300 ml/½ pt/1¼ cups **apple juice**

Salt and freshly ground black pepper

3 **tomatoes**, skinned and sliced

1   Preheat the slow cooker on High.

2   Heat the butter or margarine in a frying pan and fry the courgettes quickly until lightly browned. Transfer to the slow cooker.

3   In the same fat, fry the garlic and onion gently until transparent. Add the cornflour, then carefully stir in the apple juice. Season with salt and pepper, stir in the tomatoes and bring to the boil, stirring continuously. Pour the sauce over the courgettes.

4   Cook on Low for 4–6 hours until the courgettes are tender but still have a slight bite.

leek & cider hotpot

6   **15** MINS   **6-10** hrs LOW

50 g/2 oz/¼ cup **butter or margarine**

100 g/4 oz **bacon**, rinded and chopped

900 g/2 lb **leeks**, chopped

2 **eating (dessert) apples**, peeled, cored and sliced

600 ml/1 pt/2½ cups **dry cider**

45 ml/3 tbsp **plain (all-purpose) flour**

Chef's note

The flavour combination of leeks and cider really do go hand-in-hand. This hotpot would make a lovely accompaniment to a pork-based dish, or could be a main course in itself, served with steamed vegetables.

1   Preheat the slow cooker on High.

2   Heat the butter or margarine in a large frying pan and fry the bacon for 3 minutes. Stir in the leeks and apples and toss together well.

3   Mix a little of the cider with the flour to make a smooth paste, then blend in the remaining cider. Add to the pan and bring to the boil, stirring continuously. Transfer to the slow cooker.

4   Cook on Low for 6–10 hours.

freezing tip
• Freeze in small quantities and use as required.

tuna-stuffed marrow

6   **10 MINS**   **8-10 hrs LOW**

200 g/7 oz/small can of **tuna**, drained and flaked

1 **onion**, finely chopped

60 ml/4 tbsp **cooked long-grain rice**

15 ml/1 tbsp **chopped fresh parsley**

Juice of 1 **lemon**

Salt and freshly ground black pepper

1 **marrow (squash)**

25 g/1 oz/2 tbsp **butter or margarine**

300 ml/½ pt/1¼ cups **boiling water**

Chef's note

Marrows are often plentiful and extremely affordable when they are in season in late summer and early autumn. Their own flavour is rather understated but the flesh absorbs that of the foods it is cooked with. This is a marrow recipe that is best served hot with tomato sauce as a main or side dish.

1   Preheat the slow cooker on High.

2   Mix the tuna with the onion, rice, parsley and lemon juice and season with salt and pepper.

3   Cut the ends off the marrow so it will stand upright in the slow cooker, then scoop out the seeds. Fill the marrow with the mixture and wrap in buttered foil. Stand the marrow in the slow cooker and pour the water around.

4   Cook on Low for 8–10 hours.

greek mushrooms

8   **10** MINS   **2-3** hrs LOW

Chef's note

This is another of those recipes where the flavour of finished product is so much more than you would expect from the simplicity of the ingredients. It goes particularly well with chicken or just about any barbecued meats or fish.

30 ml/2 tbsp **oil**

1 **onion**, finely chopped

1 **garlic clove**, crushed

450 g/1 lb **button mushrooms**

225 g/8 oz **chestnut mushrooms**

400 g/14 oz/large can of **chopped tomatoes**

Salt and freshly ground black pepper

15 ml/1 tbsp **chopped fresh parsley**

1   Preheat the slow cooker on High.

2   Heat the oil in a frying pan and fry the onion and garlic gently until transparent. Add the mushrooms and tomatoes and season with salt and pepper. Bring to the boil, then transfer to the slow cooker.

3   Cook on Low for 2–3 hours.

4   Stir in the parsley before serving.

marinated mushrooms

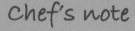

Chef's note

Here mushrooms are stewed in a mixture of butter, sugar and soy sauce to really bring out their flavour. Serve as a side dish to accompany a cold lunch, or as part of a party spread.

8

15 MINS

6-8 hrs LOW

250 ml/8 fl oz/1 cup **soy sauce**

250 ml/8 fl oz/1 cup **water**

100 g/4 oz/½ cup **butter**

200 g/7 oz/scant 1 cup **white sugar**

450 g/1 lb **fresh mushrooms**, stems removed

1 Preheat the slow cooker on Low.

2 Mix together the soy sauce, water and butter in a saucepan over a low heat. Stir until the butter has melted, then gradually mix in the sugar until it has dissolved completely.

3 Place the mushrooms in a slow cooker and cover with the soy sauce mixture.

4 Cook on Low for 6–8 hours, stirring approximately every hour. Chill before serving.

baked cheese onions

4

10 MINS

6-8 hrs LOW

4 **onions**

100 g/4 oz/1 cup **strong cheese,** grated

50 g/2 oz/1 cup **fresh breadcrumbs**

Salt and freshly ground black pepper

150 ml/¼ ml/⅔ cup **hot vegetable stock**

Chef's note

Briefly boiling the onions softens them so that their cores should slip out fairly easily. You could use the cores for another recipe, or chop them to add to this stuffing mixture. Serve as a side dish or a main course with salad.

1   Preheat the slow cooker on High.

2   Peel the onions and cut the bases flat so that they stand upright. Place in a pan, cover with water, bring to the boil, then boil for 3 minutes. Drain well and remove the cores.

3   Mix together the cheese and breadcrumbs and season with salt and pepper. Mix in the chopped onion cores, if using. Stuff into the centres of the onions, pressing down firmly. Stand the onions in the slow cooker and pour the stock over.

4   Cook on Low for 6–8 hours.

italian stuffed peppers

4 | **15 MINS** | **5-8 hrs LOW**

Chef's note

Stuffed peppers are a really delightful dish but it can be tricky to get the timing right when cooking them conventionally. In the slow cooker the pepper casing and the filling reach perfection at exactly the same time! Serve as a side dish or a main course with salad.

50 g/2 oz **quick-cook thin macaroni**

Salt

30 ml/2 tbsp **oil**

1 **onion**, diced

1 **garlic clove**, crushed

450 g/1 lb **minced (ground) Quorn**

30 ml/2 tbsp **plain (all-purpose) flour**

15 ml/1 tbsp **tomato purée (paste)**

15 ml/1 tbsp **tomato ketchup (catsup)**

150 ml/¼ pt/⅔ cup **vegetable stock**

100 g/4 oz **button mushrooms** diced

5 ml/1 tsp **dried mixed herbs**

4 **large green or red (bell) peppers**

150 ml/¼ pt/⅔ cup **boiling wat**

1   Preheat the slow cooker on High.

2   Boil the macaroni in lightly salted water until just tender. Drain.

3   Meanwhile, heat the oil in a frying pan and fry the onion and garlic until transparent.

4   Add the Quorn and continue to cook, stirring, for 3 minutes. Stir in the flour, tomato purée, tomato ketchup and stock. Bring to the boil and boil until thickened, stirring continuously. Add the mushrooms, herbs and drained macaroni.

5   Remove the stalk and cut the cap from the top of each pepper. Remove the seeds and membranes. Fill the peppers with the mixture and stand them in the slow cooker, without allowing them to touch the sides. Pour the water around the peppers and add a pinch of salt.

6   Cook on Low for 5–8 hours.

cheese & onion potatoes

4

15 MINS

8-9 hrs LOW

Chef's note

This is a lovely, rich dish in which slices of potato are layered with a mixture of cheese, onion and bacon. You are very unlikely to have any left over for next day! Omit the bacon for a vegetarian dish.

25 g/1 oz/2 tbsp **butter or margarine**

100 g/4 oz **streaky bacon**, rinded and chopped

1 **onion**, finely chopped

1 **garlic clove**, crushed

100 g/4 oz/1 cup **Cheddar cheese**, grated

15 ml/1 tbsp **chopped fresh parsley**

Salt and freshly ground black pepper

900 g/2 lb **potatoes**, thinly sliced

450 ml/¾ pt/2 cups **milk**

2 **eggs**, beaten

1 Rub the butter or margarine inside the slow cooker pot, then preheat on High.

2 Fry the bacon in a frying pan until crisp. Remove with a slotted spoon.

3 Fry the onion in the bacon fat until just beginning to soften, then remove from the heat and stir in the cooked bacon, the garlic, cheese and parsley and season with salt and pepper.

4 Arrange a layer of potatoes in the base of the slow cooker and sprinkle with salt and pepper. Cover with a layer of the cheese and onion mixture, then repeat until all the ingredients have been used up, finishing with a layer of cheese.

5 Heat the milk but do not allow it to boil. Beat in the eggs, then pour over the potatoes.

6 Cook on Low for 8–9 hours.

winter potato casserole

4-6

15 MINS

6-8 hrs LOW

Steamed vegetables

Chef's note

Who would think that the humble potato could create such a warming, comforting casserole to enjoy on a cold winter's day? You could use condensed cream of chicken or celery soup instead of chicken for a vegetarian option.

50 g/2 oz/¼ cup **butter or margarine**

1 **small onion**, finely chopped

1 **garlic clove**, crushed

1 **carrot**, chopped

1 **celery stick**, finely chopped

450 g/1 lb **potatoes**, diced

2.5 ml/½ tsp **ground mace**

Salt and freshly ground black pepper

300 g/11 oz/medium can of **condensed cream of chicken soup**

150 ml/¼ pt/⅔ cup **water**

1   Preheat the slow cooker on High.

2   Heat the butter or margarine in a large frying pan and fry the onion, garlic, carrot, celery and potatoes for 5 minutes. Season with the mace and salt and pepper.

3   Mix together the soup and water, pour into the pan and bring to the boil, stirring continuously. Transfer to the slow cooker.

4   Cook on Low for 6–8 hours.

5   Serve as a main course with steamed vegetables.

pepper & nut rice

4 **15** MINS **6-8** hrs LOW

Chef's note

A vegetarian dish that not only tastes wonderful but is also full of goodness from the protein-packed nuts. It can be served as a side dish but also makes a nutritious main meal with a salad.

15 ml/1 tbsp **olive oil**

1 **onion**, finely chopped

225 g/8 oz/1 cup **easy-cook long-grain rice**

1 **red (bell) pepper**, seeded and chopped

50 g/2 oz/½ cup **walnuts**, coarsely chopped

50 g/2 oz/½ cup **almonds**, coarsely chopped

50 g/2 oz/½ cup **peanuts**, coarsely chopped

50 g/2 oz/½ cup **sultanas (golden raisins)**

300 ml/½ pt/1¼ cups **vegetable stock**

Salt and freshly ground black pepper

1   Preheat the slow cooker on High.

2   Heat the oil in a frying pan and fry the onion until transparent. Stir in all the remaining ingredients, seasoning with salt and pepper. Transfer to the slow cooker.

3   Cook on Low for 6–8 hrs.

macaroni cheese

4 **15** MINS **3-4** hrs LOW Grilled tomatoes

Chef's note

For many people, macaroni cheese was their first introduction to cooking – perhaps when they were at school or had to cater economically for a student household. It is so easy to make in the slow cooker and guaranteed to be successful. Serve as a side dish or main course.

15 g/1 oz/2 tbsp **butter or margarine**

175 g/6 oz/**quick-cook macaroni**

Salt and freshly ground black pepper

300 ml/½ pt/1¼ cups **white sauce** (see page 52)

175 g/6 oz/1½ cups **Cheddar cheese**, grated

A large pinch of **cayenne**

1   Rub the inside of the slow cooker with the butter or margarine, then preheat on High.

2   Bring a large pan of lightly salted water to the boil, add the macaroni and stir well as it returns to the boil. Boil rapidly for 2 minutes, then drain well.

3   Make the white sauce, then remove from the heat and stir in three-quarters of the cheese. Season with cayenne, salt and pepper. Mix the macaroni with the sauce and transfer to the slow cooker. Sprinkle with the remaining cheese.

4   Cook on Low for 3–4 hours.

5   Serve with grilled tomatoes.

desserts & cakes

Those delightful nursery puddings need no longer b
just memories of childhood. They can easily b
adapted for slow cooking and come out perfect
every time.

Slow-cooked fruit is something special. Its flavour
gently developed within the pot while the fruit remai
beautifully whole for serving. Or you can use the slo
cooker to make pie, pudding and crumble fillin
while you are busy with other tasks.

Delicate desserts, such as egg custard, that requi
long, slow cooking are ideal for the slow cooker
there is no danger of them overcooking and spoilin

Sponge puddings can be frozen raw or cooked but su
puddings are best frozen raw. Cooked fruits can al
be frozen, as can pie fillings. Leftover sponge puddi
can be frozen, then covered with foil in an ovenpro
dish and reheated in the slow cooker surrounded wi
water on Low for 1–2 hours. Egg custards and simil
puddings are not suitable for freezing.

Dessert tips

- Dried fruit must be covered with liquid in order to cook evenly.

- Fill steamed pudding basins only two-thirds full and make a pleat in the greaseproof (waxed) paper to allow space for the pudding to rise. Pour boiling water around the puddings to start them off well, and cook them on High.

- When adapting your own recipes, remember that fruit will require less cooking liquid.

orange rice pudding

6

5 MINS

6-8 hrs LOW

Chef's note

What could be easier to prepare and more guaranteed to emerge from the slow cooker creamy-rich and with the delightful tang of orange? What pudding could possibly be more popular?

25 g/1 oz/2 tbsp **butter or margarine**

900 ml/1½ pts/3¾ cups **milk**

150 ml/1/4 pt/⅔ cup **evaporated milk**

100 g/4 oz/½ cup **short-grain pudding rice**

50 g/2 oz/¼ cup **caster (superfine) sugar**

Grated zest and juice of 1 **orange**

A few drops of **vanilla essence (extract)**

1 Grease the inside of the slow cooker with the butter or margarine, then preheat on High.

2 Place all the remaining ingredients in the slow cooker and mix well.

3 Cook on Low for 6–8 hours.

almond rhubarb pudding

4

15 MINS

3-4 hrs HIGH

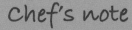

Chef's note

Rhubarb is a very old plant; it is recorded as having been grown for medicinal and culinary purposes in ancient China, giving it a nearly five thousand year history. It was even the subject of almost fanatical research from the Renaissance until the last century!

100 g/4 oz/½ cup **butter** or **margarine**, plus extra for greasing

450 g/1 lb **rhubarb**, cut into 2.5 cm/1 in pieces

45 ml/3 tbsp **caster (superfine) sugar**

100 g/4 oz/½ cup **soft brown sugar**

2 **eggs**, beaten

10 ml/2 tsp **almond essence (extract)**

175 g/6 oz/1½ cups **self-raising flour**

15 ml/1 tbsp **cocoa (unsweetened chocolate) powder**

5 ml/1 tsp **grated nutmeg**

1   Lightly grease the inside of the slow cooker, then preheat on High.

2   Arrange the rhubarb in the base of the slow cooker and sprinkle with the caster sugar.

3   Cream together the butter or margarine and brown sugar until light and fluffy. Gradually beat in the eggs and almond essence. Mix together the flour, cocoa and nutmeg, then fold into the mixture.

4   Spread the mixture over the rhubarb and cover gently with a piece of buttered greaseproof (waxed) paper, buttered-side down.

5   Cook on High for 3–4 hours.

gooseberry pie with walnuts

4   **15** MINS   **3-4** hrs HIGH

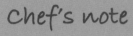
350 g/12 oz **gooseberries**

Butter for greasing

50 g/2 oz/¼ cup **caster (superfine) sugar**

25 g/1 oz/¼ cup **walnuts**, chopped

For the topping

100 g/4 oz/1 cup **self-raising flour**

50 g/2 oz/½ cup **shredded suet**

25 g/1 oz/2 tbsp **caster (superfine) sugar**

60 ml/4 tbsp **milk**

Whipped cream and a few **chopped walnuts** to decorate

1   Preheat the slow cooker on High.

2   Arrange the gooseberries in a lightly buttered ovenproof dish that fits inside the slow cooker. Arrange the gooseberries in the dish and sprinkle with the sugar and walnuts.

3   To make the topping, mix together the flour, suet and sugar. Mix in the milk to make a firm dough. Roll out on a lightly floured board to a round that fits the dish. Lay the dough on the gooseberries and cover with buttered foil. Stand the dish in the slow cooker and surround with sufficient boiling water to come half-way up the sides of the dish.

4   Cook on High for 3–4 hours.

5   Serve decorated with whipped cream and walnuts.

apricot bread & butter pud

4-6   **10 MINS**   **4-6 hrs LOW**

Chef's note

Bread pudding is always goes down well, and this is a more elegant take on the usual recipes. Almond essence is very concentrated, so you will need only a little to enhance the flavour of the custard.

8 **thin slices of bread**, crusts removed

25 g/1 oz/2 tbsp **butter or margarine**, plus extra for greasing

400 g/14 oz/1 large can of **apricots**, drained

30 ml/2 tbsp **caster (superfine) sugar**

3 **eggs**, beaten

A few drops of **almond essence (extract)**

450 m/¾ pt/2 cups **milk**

1 Preheat the slow cooker on High.

2 Spread the bread with the butter and cut into convenient-sized pieces to fit into your chosen dish. Use about three-quarters of the bread, buttered-side down, to line an ovenproof dish that fits inside the slow cooker.

3 Reserve a few apricots for decoration, then chop the remainder finely and spread over the bread. Arrange the remaining bread slices on top.

4 Beat together the sugar, eggs and almond essence.

5 Warm the milk to lukewarm, then pour on to the eggs. Pour over the bread. Cover securely with buttered foil, then stand the dish in the slow cooker and surround with sufficient boiling water to come half-way up the sides of the dish.

6 Cook on Low for 4–6 hours.

7 Decorate the pudding with the reserved apricots before serving.

lemon sponge with almonds

4

15 MINS

6-8 hrs HIGH

Chef's note

Lemon and almonds is another marriage made in heaven! A lovely light, spongy pudding to serve with whipped cream, ice-cream or custard.

50 g/2 oz/½ cup **plain (all-purpose) flour**

2.5 ml/½ tsp **baking powder**

2.5 ml/½ tsp **ground cinnamon**

50 g/2 oz/½ cup **quick-cook rolled oats**

3 ml/2 tbsp **chopped almonds**

75 g/3 oz/⅓ cup **butter or margarine**, plus extra for greasing

100 g/4 oz/½ cup **soft brown sugar**

1 **egg**, beaten

Grated zest and juice of 1 **lemon**

30 ml/2 tbsp **milk**

1   Preheat the slow cooker on High.

2   Mix together the flour, baking powder and cinnamon. Stir in the oats and almonds.

3   Beat together the butter or margarine and sugar until light and fluffy.

4   Lightly mix together the egg, lemon zest and 15 ml/1 tbsp of the lemon juice, then beat into the butter mixture a little at a time. Fold in the flour, then add enough of the milk to make a soft, dropping consistency.

5   Spoon the mixture into a greased 600 ml/1 pt/2½ cup pudding basin and cover with lightly greased foil. Stand the basin in the slow cooker and surround with sufficient boiling water to come half-way up the sides of the basin.

6   Cook on High for 6–8 hours.

orange rhubarb with ginger

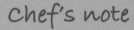

Chef's note

There are some strange incidents in rhubarb's long history. In 1620 a Chinese emperor was miraculously cured of a severe illness following a 'joyful time' with four beautiful women who arrived bearing rhubarb!

4

5 MINS

4-6 hrs LOW

450 g/1 lb **rhubarb**, cut into 2.5 cm/1 in lengths

150 ml/¼ pt/⅔ cup **water**

60 ml/4 tbsp **caster (superfine) sugar**

Grated zest and juice of 1 **orange**

90 ml/6 tbsp **whipped cream**

15 ml/1 tbsp **preserved stem ginger in syrup**, thinly sliced

1 Preheat the slow cooker on High.

2 Place the rhubarb, water, sugar and orange zest and juice in the slow cooker and mix together well.

3 Cook on Low for 4–6 hours.

4 Transfer to a serving dish and chill until ready to serve.

5 Serve chilled, decorated with the whipped cream and ginger slices.

syrup suet pudding

4　　**10 MINS**　　**3-4 hrs HIGH**

100 g/4 oz/1 cup **self-raising flour**

A pinch of **salt**

50 g/2 oz/¼ cup **caster (superfine) sugar**

50 g/2 oz/½ cup **shredded suet**

1 **egg**, beaten

45 ml/3 tbsp **milk**

60 ml/4 tbsp **golden (light corn) syrup**

Butter for greasing

This nursery-style pudding is an all-time favourite for many, young and old alike. Using the slow cooker means you won't have a hot and steamy kitchen for hours on end.

1 Preheat the slow cooker on High.

2 Mix together the flour, salt, sugar and suet. Stir in the egg and enough of the milk to make a soft, dropping consistency. Spoon the syrup into a buttered 600 ml/1 pt/2½ cup pudding basin, then carefully top with the sponge mixture and cover with buttered foil. Stand the basin in the slow cooker and surround with sufficient boiling water to come half-way up the sides of the basin.

3 Cook on High for 3–4 hours.

4 Invert on to a warmed serving dish to serve.

baked apples with stuffing

4   **10** MINS   **4-6** hrs LOW

Chef's note

Try this recipe in the autumn when cooking apples are abundant both from the garden and in the shops. The flavours of the filling and the apple 'melt' into each other during the long cooking to create a deliciously sweet treat.

4 **cooking (tart) apples**

25 g/1 oz/3 tbsp **raisins**

25 g/1 oz/3 tbsp **sultanas (golden raisins)**

50 g/2 oz/¼ cup **soft brown sugar**

15 ml/1 tbsp **hazelnuts (filberts)**, chopped

A pinch of **ground cinnamon**

75 ml/5 tbsp **water**

1   Preheat the slow cooker on High.

2   Core the apples and peel a strip around the 'equator' of each apple.

3   Mix together the raisins, sultanas, sugar, hazelnuts and cinnamon and press into the centres of the apples, piling any extra on top. Place the apples in the slow cooker and spoon the water around.

4   Cook on Low for 4–6 hours.

christmas pudding

6   **20** MINS   **12** hrs HIGH

Chef's note

Don't be put off by the rather long list of ingredients because making your own Christmas pudding couldn't be simpler – and will be incomparably moister, fruitier and more delicious than any you could buy from a shop.

50 g/2 oz/½ cup **plain (all-purpose) flour**

2.5 ml/½ tsp **mixed (apple-pie) spice**

2.5 ml/½ tsp **ground cinnamon**

2.5 ml/½ tsp **grated nutmeg**

50 g/2 oz/1 cup **fresh breadcrumbs**

150 g/5 oz/1¼ cups **shredded suet**

100 g/4 oz/½ cup **soft brown sugar**

175 g/6 oz/1 cup **raisins**

175 g/6 oz/1 cup **sultanas (golden raisins)**

25 g/1 oz/3 tbsp **chopped mixed (candied) peel**

25 g/1 oz/¼ cup **ground almonds**

2 large **eggs**, beaten

Finely grated zest and juice of 1 **orange**

15 ml/1 tbsp **black treacle (molasses)**

15 ml/1 tbsp **brandy or dry sherry**

2.5 ml/½ tsp **almond essence (extract)**

60 ml/4 tbsp **beer**

Butter for greasing

1 Preheat the slow cooker on High.

2 Mix together all the dry ingredients in a large bowl. Beat the eggs with the remaining ingredients in a separate bowl, then stir well into the flour mixture. Spoon the mixture into a greased 1 litre/1¾ pt/4¼ cup pudding basin and cover securely with buttered foil. Stand the basin in the slow cooker and surround with boiling water to come half-way up the sides of the basin.

3 Cook on High for 12 hours.

reheating tip
• Ideally, make your Christmas pudding in October and then leave to mature in a cool, dark place. To serve, preheat the slow cooker on High for 20 minutes. Place the pudding in the slow cooker and surround with boiling water, as before. Cook on Low for about 6 hours, or on High for about 4 hours.

baked custard

4

5 MINS

4-6 hrs LOW

Chef's note

Slow cooking is guaranteed to produce a perfect, worry-free baked custard. Remember that vanilla essence is very concentrated, so you will need to add only a few drops.

4 **eggs**

50 g/2 oz/¼ cup **caster (superfine) sugar**

600 ml/1 pt/2½ cups **milk**

A few drops of **vanilla essence (extract)**

A little **grated nutmeg**

1   Preheat the slow cooker on High.

2   Blend together the eggs and sugar.

3   Warm the milk to lukewarm, then pour it on to the eggs and add the vanilla essence. Pour the custard into a 1 litre/ 1¾ pt/4¼ cup ovenproof dish and sprinkle with nutmeg, then cover with foil. Stand the dish in the slow cooker and surround with sufficient boiling water to come half-way up the sides of the dish.

4   Cook on Low for 4–6 hours until a knife inserted in the centre comes out clean.

crème caramel

We give a guide time of 5–6 hours here, but the cooking time may vary depending on the type and size of dish used. The cooked custard should be just firm and set so check after 4 hours (don't leave the slow cooker uncovered longer than absolutely necessary) and give it more time if needed.

4-6 **10** MINS **5-6** hrs LOW

100 g/4 oz/½ cup **caster (superfine) sugar**

150 ml/¼ pt/⅔ cup **water**

600 ml/1 pt/2½ cups **milk**

4 **eggs**

A few drops of **vanilla essence (extract)**

1   Preheat the slow cooker on High.

2   To make the caramel, heat 30 ml/2 tbsp of the sugar with the water in a small pan until the sugar has dissolved. Bring to the boil, then boil rapidly until it turns golden. Pour into a warmed soufflé dish and allow to cool.

3   Beat together the milk, eggs, vanilla essence and remaining sugar. Bring to blood heat, then strain on to the caramel. Cover with foil, then stand the dish in the slow cooker and surround with sufficient boiling water to come half-way up the sides of the dish.

4   Cook on Low for 5–6 hours.

5   Leave to cool, then chill for several hours. Ease the custard away from the sides of the dish before turning out to serve.

blueberry & apple crumble

6

10 MINS

3-4 hrs HIGH

Ice-cream

1.5 kg/3 lb **cooking (tart) apples**, peeled, cored and sliced

225 g/8 oz fresh **blueberries**

100 g/4 oz/½ cup **caster (superfine) sugar**

30 ml/2 tbsp **lemon juice**

15 ml/1 tbsp **cornflour** (cornstarch)

2.5 ml/½ tsp **ground cinnamon**

For the topping:

100 g/4 oz/½ cup **muscovado sugar**

75 g/6 oz/¾ cup **rolled oats**

60 ml/4 tbsp **desiccated (shredded) coconut**

50 g/2 oz/¼ cup **butter**, chopped into small chunks

1   Mix together the apples, blueberries and lemon juice in the slow cooker.

2   Mix together the cornflour and cinnamon and stir into the mixture until well blended.

3   Mix together the topping ingredients and rub through your fingertips so the butter is blended into the mix. Sprinkle over the fruit.

4   Cover tightly and cook on High for 3–4 hours.

5   Serve with ice-cream.

slow-cooked gingerbread

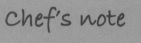
Chef's note

Gingerbread is another treat often associated with bonfire night, presumably for the warming qualities of ginger. But this great cake with a sticky glaze can be enjoyed mid-morning or at teatime any time of year.

225 g/8 oz/1 cup **dark muscovado sugar**

175 g/6 oz/¾ cup **butter or margarine**, plus extra for greasing

350 g/12 oz/1 cup **golden (light corn) syrup**

450 g/1 lb **plain (all-purpose) flour**

5 ml/1 tsp **salt**

15 ml/1 tbsp **ground ginger**

10 ml/2 tsp **baking powder**

1 **egg**

300 ml/½ pt/1¼ cups **milk**

50 g/2 oz/⅓ cup **glacé (candied) cherries**, chopped, or chopped **mixed (candied) peel**

50 g/2 oz/¼ cup **caster (superfine) sugar**

30 ml/2 tbsp **water**

1   Preheat the slow cooker on High.

2   Melt together the muscovado sugar, butter or margarine and syrup gently in a non-stick pan until the sugar has dissolved. Allow to cool.

3   Place the flour, salt, ginger and baking powder in a bowl and make a well in the centre. Pour in the melted mixture and mix until smooth. Pour into a greased 18 cm/7 in round cake tin and sprinkle with the glacé cherries or mixed peel. Cover with greased foil and stand the tin in the slow cooker. Surround with sufficient boiling water to come half-way up the sides of the tin.

4   Cook on High for 6–8 hours.

5   Turn the gingerbread out of the tin. Blend together the caster sugar and water and brush over the top of the hot gingerbread. Leave to cool.

freezing tip
- Interleave slices of gingerbread with greaseproof (waxed) paper and wrap securely in foil to freeze so you can use individual servings.

nut & banana bread

6-8 **15** MINS **2-3** hrs HIGH

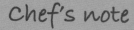

Chef's note

A really tasty fruit-and-nut bread, as ideal for picnics and in the lunchbox as it is at teatime. Serve sliced and buttered.

175 g/6 oz/1½ cups **self-raising flour**

A pinch of **salt**

2.5 ml/½ tsp **grated nutmeg**

75 g/3 oz/⅓ cup **butter or margarine**, plus extra for greasing

100 g/4 oz/½ cup **muscovado sugar**

50 g/2 oz/⅓ cup **sultanas (golden raisins)**

50 g/2 oz/½ cup **chopped mixed nuts**

3 **ripe bananas**, chopped

2 **eggs**, beaten

1   Preheat the slow cooker on High.

2   Mix together the flour, salt and nutmeg in a bowl, then rub in the butter or margarine until the mixture resembles breadcrumbs. Stir in the sugar, sultanas and nuts.

3   Mash the bananas until soft, then stir into the eggs. Mix into the dry ingredients until well blended. Spoon into a greased 18 cm/7 in cake tin and cover with greased foil. Place in the slow cooker and surround with sufficient boiling water to come half-way up the sides of the tin.

4   Cook on High for 2–3 hours.

freezing tip
• This will freeze well for up to 3 months.

chocolate cake with butter icing

6-8   **15** MINS   **3-4** hrs HIGH

Chef's note

This is a delightfully indulgent yet light treat with a rich and smooth chocolate filling and topping. Isn't chocolate cake everyone's teatime favourite?

For the cake

15 ml/1 tbsp **cocoa (unsweetened chocolate) powder**

30 ml/2 tbsp **hot water**

100 g/4 oz/½ cup **butter or margarine**, plus extra for greasing

100 g/4 oz/½ cup **caster (superfine) sugar**

2 **eggs**, beaten

100 g/4 oz/1 cup **self-raising flour**

For the icing (frosting)

30 ml/2 tbsp **cocoa (unsweetened chocolate) powder**

30 ml/2 tbsp **hot water**

225 g/8 oz/1⅓ cups **icing (confectioners') sugar**

75 g/3 oz/½ cup **butter or margarine**, softened

45 ml/3 tbsp **milk**

1   Preheat the slow cooker on High.

2   To make the cake, blend the cocoa to a paste with the hot water, then leave to cool.

3   Cream together the butter or margarine and sugar until light and fluffy. Beat in the cocoa mixture, then beat in the eggs a little at a time alternately with a little of the flour. Gently fold in the remaining flour. Spoon the mixture into a greased 18 cm/7 in cake tin and cover with foil. Stand the tin in the slow cooker and surround with sufficient boiling water to come half-way up the sides of the tin.

4   Cook on High for 3–4 hours.

5   To make the icing, blend the cocoa and hot water to a paste, then leave to cool.

6   Gradually beat the icing sugar and cocoa mixture into the butter or margarine, adding enough of the milk to make a smooth but fairly stiff butter icing.

7   Halve the cooled cake horizontally, then sandwich together with half the icing. Spread the remaining icing on top.

pineapple upside down cake

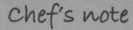

4

15 MINS

4-5 hrs
1 HIGH +
3-4 LOW

Chef's note

A deliciously moist and spongy indulgence. Once cooked, turn it out of the dish and serve warm as a dessert with ice-cream or cream or cold as a cake.

50 g/2 oz/¼ cup **butter** or **margarine**

100 g/4 oz/½ cup **soft brown sugar**

400 g/14 oz/large can of **pineapple slices**, drained

A few **glacé (candied) cherries**

For the sponge

175 g/6 oz/¾ cup **butter or margarine**

175 g/6 oz/¾ cup **caster (superfine) sugar**

3 **eggs**, beaten

175 g/6 oz/1½ cups **self-raising flour**

30 ml/2 tbsp **milk**

1   Place the butter or margarine in the slow cooker to melt and preheat on High.

2   Stir in the sugar, then arrange the pineapple slices and cherries over the base of the dish.

3   To make the sponge, cream together the butter or margarine and sugar, then gradually beat in the eggs, a little at a time, and fold in the flour. Add enough of the milk to make a soft, dropping consistency. Spoon the sponge mixture over the pineapple and topping.

4   Cook on High for 1 hour, then on Low for 3–4 hours.

index